LIGHTEN UP!

Free Yourself from Clutter

Michelle Passoff

LIGHTEN UP!

Free Yourself from Clutter

HarperPerennial
A Division of HarperCollinsPublishers

HarperCollins books may be purchased for educational, business, or sales promotional use. For information please write: Special Markets Department, HarperCollins Publishers, Inc., 10 East 53rd Street, New York, NY 10022.

FIRST EDITION

Designed by Elina D. Nudelman

Library of Congress Cataloging-in-Publication Data

Passoff, Michelle.
    Lighten Up! : free yourself from clutter / Michelle Passoff.
        p.   cm.
    ISBN 0-06-095265-2
    1. House cleaning.   I. Title.
    TX324.P37   1998
    648' .5—dc21   97-45040

98 99 00 01 02 ❖/RRD 10 9 8 7 6 5 4 3 2 1

I dedicate this book with love to the memory
of my father and brother
Daniel Passoff
and
Todd Lewis Passoff, M.D.

Contents

Acknowledgments

Clutter cleaning is about acquiring an ability to rely solely upon oneself to create an environment that is nurturing and supportive. It does not depend on someone else. Writing a book on the subject of clutter, however, required stepping out way beyond my personal space to include others. I was always mindful of the importance of extending what I considered most sacred about living clutter free to these relationships and the making of this book. I felt it would take this type of atmosphere to foster the proper presentation of the unique perspectives that you will find in these pages so that they could reach the broadest possible audience. Achieving this was not without its challenges. But, in the end, I am happy to have so many people to thank for the fact that not only has this book arrived in great form, but that the journey to get here has been amazingly expansive.

First, I would like to thank the hundreds of students and

private clients who attended my classes and retained my services for giving as much, or more, to me than I gave to them. I am grateful that they considered what I taught valuable, otherwise I would not have had a reason to continue. To be able to say that you love your clients and that they have given you so much pleasure and encouragement is indeed an accomplishment, and I owe my success to them. To all of you, thank you for allowing me into one of the most intimate areas of your life.

I owe a great debt of gratitude to Anne Raver of the *New York Times* for giving me my big break. Even though I spent twenty years as a media specialist in the public relations business before becoming a clutter consultant, never have I had an experience of the power of the press quite like the one I've had since you made my clutter work and me a part of "all the news that's fit to print." From the bottom of my heart, I thank you for opening up so much space in my life.

To William Clark, the agent who breathed life into this project, thank you for your great vision, open ears, and kind heart. I will always treasure our relationship.

Megan Newman of HarperCollins has been there right from the beginning with nothing but enthusiasm for this project. I hold being a good communicator in the highest esteem and consider it to be one of your greatest qualities. Thank you for giving me a chance. I am also grateful to John Wing at HarperCollins. Thank you for bringing your marketing genius and support to this book.

Anne Halpin has spent a good part of every day for one entire year in the trenches with me helping to give structure to my thoughts and form to my words. Thank you for all of your hard work and for causing me to create.

Thanks to Adele Heyman at The Open Center in New York for so readily being the first to have me teach "Lighten Up! Free Yourself from Clutter" in a holistic context. Thanks to Stephen Breen at Interface in Boston, Lily Gaines at the Oasis

Center in Chicago, and Donna Olden-Tanner at Oakwood Farm Retreat in Selma, Indiana for allowing me to bring my work beyond the Hudson River and for sharing a commitment to the possibility for humankind. Thanks to Craig Jones for the clutter song and for bringing me to Los Angeles.

My deepest appreciation to Deborah Durham of Spokespersons Plus Network for making my dream of the marketing of this book come true.

Thank you to my mother, Diane Passoff, for giving me life and for being my first and most important teacher. Many thanks to my teachers at Landmark Education Corporation, Marilyn Graman, Glenn and Christina Sirlin, Gerry Goodman, Cia Ricco, and The American Woman's Economic Development Corporation. Special thanks to Tamara Engel for providing me with so many critical insights and to Dr. Blandine Laferrere, Amy Funkhauser, Meredith Gunsberg, Marilyn Migliore, Kathy Nonas, and Henie Simon at St. Luke's-Roosevelt Hospital for bringing so much vitality to my education about the physical body during the process of writing this book.

Many thanks to Rabbi Joseph Gelberman for having me understand the profound meaning of acceptance and to Gurumayi Chidvilasananda for showing me that the answers lie within.

Thanks to Deborah Green and Judy Caparelli for starting the whole thing. Thanks to Moira Walter, one of the best friends a girl can have; Gaye Carleton of Carleton and Company public relations for her friendship and professional input; Stephen Schmidt for sharing his experience as an author, for his encouragement, and for being a good buddy; and to Tantra Maat for being a friend, teacher, and partner in exploring all realms of existence. Thanks to Malik for the soulful journey, memorable moments, and practical advice at the right time. Thanks to Barry Zaid for creating my first seminar with me on a napkin over lunch; to Elli and Randy Fordyce for giving me my first computer so I could start writing; and to Leonard and

Sarah Marsh, perfect strangers, who gave me the miracle gift of a car so I had the room I needed to move along the road to publish.

Special thanks to Rosalind, Arnold, Vicky, and Roger Dubin for adopting me into their family and to Nancy Blum Feinglass, Kathy Connolly, Susan Sidor, Jane Karesh, Diane Caruso, Roberta Jaret, and Rob and Yoko Boezewinkel for their friendship along the way. Thanks to Howard Finkelson, Emma Muradian, and Greg Hund for their special brand of support.

To David Stein of Pryor, Cashman, Sherman & Flynn, I cannot thank you enough for acting in my best interest. Also thanks to Stephen Beer of Rudolph and Beer, Richard Comer, and Faye Kilstein.

Many thanks to all of my friends and colleagues at Edelman Public Relations Worldwide, especially Jody Quinn, Judy Grossman, Lauren Snyder, Janice Rotchstein, and Bonnie Warschauer for permitting me the creative space to have two careers and for their support.

Last, but not least, I acknowledge myself for never losing faith and for always finding joy, even in unlikely places.

Part I

GETTING STARTED

The Beginning

If you were asked to guess what I do for a living on the basis of the messages I get on my answering machine, you might think I am a plumber, a locksmith, a doctor, or some other sort of emergency care worker. "My husband is in trouble, please call me as soon as you get in." "I just lost my job. Can you come over this afternoon?" "I was just booted out of my office space and moved my business home. Now what do I do?" "Hi, I'm calling from Boston, but my daughter just graduated from college in New York. She needs your help, and I'm willing to pay. Please call." "I'm standing on the corner of Sixty-eighth Street and Second Avenue and I can't get into my apartment. It's urgent. Here's my number."

Many of the calls and letters I get are not from just down the block. There was the letter from the mother in Florida whose teenage daughters were getting out of hand, and one from a woman in Arizona asking for advice about what to do about her aging mother. There was a call from a reporter from a popular magazine in Japan who thought a chat with me might help her fellow countrymen. There was also a call from a teenager in Connecticut whose family was moving to a smaller house; not only did he not know what to do about it, he also wanted help with his study habits. Then there was the woman from the Yukon Territory who heard about me from someone in Indiana. Do you know where the Yukon Territory is? It is practically at the end of the earth.

But clutter knows no boundaries, and clutter is my specialty. I am a clutter consultant, a profession I stumbled upon, but one to which I seem to have been called. My journey through life has been guided by a thirst to examine what I wanted my experience of being alive to be and by exploring ways to manifest it in the world. I became a serious student—working with many great teachers on issues of humanity, relationship, business, and spirituality—in my quest to have my inner and outer worlds be one. Every time I took a quantum leap in my growth, I noticed that I would clean physical clutter. Every time I clarified my thoughts and emotions or specified my desires, I would find myself creating filing systems and a wardrobe that corresponded to my interests and goals. I thought it was curious that I responded in this way to personal expansion, so I decided at one point to conduct an experiment to see whether if I reversed the process and cleaned clutter first as a way to foster growth if it would work. It did! And, it was fun. I began to make a game of exploring the relationship among oneness with myself, harmony in the world, and my physical environment.

In the early 1990s, I was winding down a twenty-year career as a public relations consultant, turning forty, and traumatized by the sudden loss of my father and the unexpected death of my brother, all within six months. In the midst of my upheaval, two friends independently called to ask me to help them with theirs. They asked me to help them clean their clutter to facilitate moving to new homes. This became an opportunity to share with them all that I had learned about clutter. I helped one friend clean closets on Monday, another friend clean up her clutter on Saturday, and by Thursday I started my business Lighten Up! Free Yourself from Clutter.

Since that time, all kinds of people have called. They were from many geographic territories, educational backgrounds, economic levels, professions, and circumstances and of all ages. They were men, women, and even children. They had a single-minded quest in common: They wanted to know how to clean up all those papers, clothes, and other paraphernalia heaped all over their living rooms, bedrooms, basements, attics, bathrooms, and offices. They seemed to have had a moment of awakening when all their stuff had reached such monumental proportions that they were thrown into a panic and their need to do something about it could not wait a minute longer. I taught them what I had learned: The future is bright without clutter in the way.

As I continued to share my outlook about clutter in private consultations and seminars in my hometown of New York City (the place I affectionately call The Clutter Capital of the World) and throughout the country, what I discovered to be effective in cleaning clutter grew and my understanding about the mysteries of the physical universe deepened. My approach focuses on getting rid of the most basic forms of clutter in the physical environment as a path toward cleaning whatever is in the way of fulfillment anywhere.

If what you are looking for is a method to file papers, a way to get your closets in better shape, and suggestions on other rooms, various kinds of clutter, and situations in which clutter can be found, you will find it here. You'll also find practical suggestions about what to do with the daily mail, nagging catalogs, an avalanche of books, and a garage that is an embarrassment to the neighborhood. I also give you information on managing time and keeping a date book so you have less stress in a day, and more.

I do not provide a set of quick fixes or easy answers,

however. I have not found that quick fixes work to give people what they really want from cleaning clutter—a lasting change in their relationship to their physical environment that leads to greater effectiveness, productivity, spontaneity, creativity, fulfillment, and peace of mind in their lives. I offer a way you can transform your ways with clutter so your environment can nurture and support you on an ongoing basis. Any kind of transformation takes work, but it is an investment that leads to an enriched experience of being alive, so it is worth it. It can make a difference in your life, the lives of those around you, and ultimately in the world.

To help you define and achieve your objectives, I borrow goal-setting, strategy-building and planning techniques from business to help you structure your clutter-cleaning endeavors so that things actually get done and you can see results. This approach is as practical as it is motivating. I suggest that you put yourself on a clutter-cleaning "diet" of sorts. In other words, I recommend that you specify a time in which you will work on a designated area of clutter and use the techniques that I suggest to clean it. Doing so will give you practice with the principles of cleaning clutter that I outline.

As most of us have come to learn, however, diets don't work. If you want to be healthy and stay in shape, you eventually have to find a way of eating and exercising that uniquely works for you and that you can integrate into your lifestyle. Likewise, once you have read this book and the clutter-cleaning diet is over, I urge you not to feel forced to follow the Lighten Up! Free Yourself from Clutter approach as if it is a set of rules. Instead, pull from it whatever you have found from your experience works and incorporate it into your own clutter-cleaning program.

You should not think that you need to make your clutter-cleaning effort a rush to the finish either because, as you will soon learn, there is no end to clutter anyway. Staying committed and working steadily over time have proved more effective. Try to make a conscious choice to bring enthusiasm to each step of the task and to realize that any forward movement is as important a part of the process as is the end result. For example, if you were writing the great American novel but first needed to learn to use the computer, learning the computer would be as much a part of the process as sitting down with words spewing forth from your infinite imagination. It could be as thrilling to learn the computer as it is to write, if you take this perspective. Both are all part of the process of completing the novel.

Part of what can make the process of cleaning fun is to become aware of the points of interest you can find on your travels through all your clutter. The highlights of the trip are that clutter cleaning is a way to discover who you really are and what you want in life, which I will show you how to do. This discovery can help your communication and relationships with other people, because if you can speak and act consistenly with who you are, you will open the space in your life for more love to abound. Finally, you can discover how you can harness the power of physical and spiritual energy in the process. I will point out how clutter cleaning unleashes this power to produce results and bring magic and miracles into your life. Whatever route through your clutter you take, I promise one miracle for each bag that you fill with what you no longer want or use and magic as a way of life if you fill it with what nurtures and supports you.

The most important thing is to get started. So let's begin. You may want to browse through the book from start to finish first. Then revisit it as you clean, reading chapters that are particularly pertinent to whatever you are working on at the time. Review the At-a-Glance sections when you need a pick-me-up. And, just for the fun of it, turn to any page in the book each time before you clean for some inspiration. Rest assured that as you work, you won't be alone. Although I may not be there physically, I will be there in spirit cheering you on. Enjoy!

1

How Did Things Get to Be Such a Mess?

Since opening my business, Lighten Up! Free Yourself from Clutter in 1991, I have conducted private consultations, seminars, and workshops in my hometown of New York and throughout the country for many hundreds of clients. Most people's approach to cleaning clutter is to ask themselves some form of one of these questions: Why am I such a mess? How did I get to be such a mess? What are the reasons for clutter? The questions seem to beg for an answer that will provide a personality, character, or psychological profile that is common to all people who have clutter.

The Lighten Up! Free Yourself from Clutter approach to cleaning clutter is not based on the need to understand your psychological and emotional composition before you start to clean. Rather, it acknowledges the value of understanding the psychological and emotional aspects of yourself to growing, but recognizes that you do not have to have all your questions about why you are the way you are and how you got to be where you are answered before you start to clean your clutter.

Although I encourage you to be open to insights that can be gained about who you are and where you are going as you clean, the Lighten Up! Free Yourself from Clutter point of departure for self-expansion is through the physical realm and everyday clutter. Since all aspects of the self are interrelated, when you begin to shift your physical environment, you will also be moved emotionally, psychologically, mentally, and spiritually. Clutter is tangible, however, which makes it an easy place to go to work on your life because it is the one aspect that you can actually get your hands on.

If, as you clean your clutter, you get stumped by a hand-me-down habit, a bad feeling, a poor attitude, or a detrimental memory that you no longer want, need, use, or love and that does not nurture and support you as you move on in your life, then, just like all other forms of clutter, do not step over it. Address it. For example, if your financial affairs are in disorder and nothing you do can bring you to straighten things out, examining your and your family's attitudes toward money may disclose useful information that can open the door. If your body and self-image are suffering along with the condition of your closets, a peek into the past can expose the raw truth about why things are disheveled. The roots of behaviors, such as the lack of discipline, laziness, rebellion, or hoarding, may be deeply implanted in a place that now has you stuck in your physical surroundings.

I am not a psychologist, and my professional experience and personal passion are rooted in the field of communication, not analysis, but I have observed that when it comes to clutter people are either exactly like or exactly the opposite of what they learned as children. If they were raised in tidy homes, they want to have the opposite type of home. If a messy environment was their breeding ground, clutter may mimic the familiar. If they grew up with too little, craving lots just in case may prevail. And if they grew up in homes of plenty, they may be prone to out-of-control purchasing.

A traumatic event in the near or distant past can leave its scars on the present in the form of clutter. I have had students and clients recount that the impact on them of adoption; death; and even in one case, incest, has been clutter.

Whether it was good or bad, you have a past—everyone does. But the past does not have to stop you from moving forward. If it does and looking into it will help you to clean your clutter, make that investigation part of the fun and games of uncovering all kinds of enlightening stuff as you clean. Seek resources to help you illuminate that area. Read books that discuss psychological aspects of yourself that you think are linked to your clutter. One of the best books I have found that explores one's relationship to "home" from a psychological perspective is Clare Cooper Marcus's *House as a Mirror of Self* (Conari Press, 1995). The book includes stories and exercises that can be useful in helping you explore how your viewpoints about home developed early on and how they play out in your life today. Or speak to a professional counselor trained in psychology. Simply spending time alone or talking to a friend may help you learn about yourself. The key is to use what you learn because when it comes to your clutter-cleaning success, action makes all the difference.

One of the first actions that you can take to clean clutter is to begin to think less in terms of how clutter cleaning links you to the past and more about how it can open the door to a new future. Trading in some old perspectives about cleaning and clutter for some new ones will get you off on the right foot and help free up some space to move ahead.

THE MIGHTY MOUSE THEORY OF CLEANING CLUTTER

Part of the Saturday morning heaven for me as a child was cartoons. There was Felix the Cat, who always had that wonderful bag of tricks. Then, there was Mighty Mouse.

Mighty Mouse used to fly across the television screen in his tights and cape with the big "M" splashed across his chest, and an announcer would boom and boast—HERE HE COMES TO SAVE THE DAY—MIIIIGHTEEEE MOUSE!

The Mighty Mouse theory of living is a good concept for kids because it is free of responsibility. In our household, Mom—just like Mighty Mouse—would always be there to save the day. Whenever I couldn't find something, I'd know who to ask—my mother. My mother always was able to locate whatever I was missing or needed. If something required mending or pressing, a purchase needed to be made for a school project, or getting to and from various activities was a must, the burden of seeing things through was always on her shoulders, not mine. I'm not of the belief that all good things must come to an end, but along with the independence of flying out of the nest came the rude awakening that my mother (and father) were no longer going to take charge of managing my life and business affairs. And Mighty Mouse was not coming to save the day.

Regardless of age, however, many of us still operate according to the Mighty Mouse theory of living. Although there are many times when I would gladly elect to be the president of the Long Live Mighty Mouse! fan club, when it comes to your success with cleaning clutter, this theory will not work. Nobody else can be responsible for cleaning your clutter but you.

All the books on clutter (including this one) that you buy will not clean your clutter for you. All the classes on clutter and all the notes you could take in them will not get the job done. If you are not the one in charge, not even hiring a personal clutter consultant or an organizational expert will help you get a handle on clutter. You have to be senior in command.

Since clutter does not go away by itself, you are going to have to take the reins and see that it gets cleaned up. Although we can now buy self-cleaning ovens and self-defrost refrigerators, the automatic clutter-cleaning machine is a long way off. Thank goodness, because to have clutter is to be human and to clean it is to delve into yourself and learn about what really counts.

Although clutter cleaning can help bring you peace, finding a way to get started can be a battle. But it does not have to be. My best advice is to find a way to relate to the task of cleaning clutter so it is not a burden, but an adventure or a challenge. As you comb through the following chapters and through your clutter, be on the lookout for the ways in which your hard-earned efforts will be the most worthwhile. Look far beyond the pile of papers on your desk and search for benefits far deeper than what you see on the surface. Try to identify what you are determined enough to have in your life, and how taking responsibility for cleaning your clutter will help you gain it. Adopt the take-the-bull-by-the-horns, pull-yourself-up-by-the-bootstraps, get-going attitude. Put yourself in the driver's seat, put the pedal to the metal, and take off.

Mighty Mouse may not be coming to save the day, but you stand to discover that you are Mighty Mouse!

ARE YOU REALLY READY TO CHANGE?

Successfully cleaning clutter implies that you are making a move in your life. Each effort you make brings you closer to your true heart's desires. But change often brings discomfort as you move away from what you know. Although being clutter free seems like a good idea, ask yourself if you are really *ready* to do the work and make the change.

Throughout the clutter-cleaning process you will be asking yourself many, many questions about what is and what is not relevant to the life you really want to be leading. Honesty is a key ingredient to success. The dream of being clutter free can come true, and the information and skills in this book can help make it happen if you take the steps. But you've got to be ready to act.

After giving a lecture on clutter, I was approached by a woman who wanted help dealing with the many piles of magazines she had stacked in her apartment. I gave her some ideas, and then it occurred to me that if she wanted to get rid of her magazines, I could help her. I had an all-day workshop coming up in just a few weeks and needed magazines for the Collage Exercise (which is presented in chapter 2 of this book) that I do during the class. I offered some free on-site counseling and said that I'd be willing to take her magazines off her hands. She hesitated and then declined the offer. She is not a horrible person because she did not seize the opportunity to receive the gift of clutter cleaning; she just was not ready.

In another instance, Jim asked me to help him because his bird was cluttering his life. Jim loves birds—exotic birds. He and his wife kept theirs in the second bedroom of their two-bedroom apartment. But they had just had a baby and did not want the baby and the bird sharing the same room.

I said, "Jim, have you thought about putting the bird in the bedroom with your wife and you?"

"Yeah," he said, "we thought of that, and we decided that we don't want the bird to be in our room."

I then suggested, "Jim, have you thought about putting the bird in the living room?"

"Yes," replied Jim. "We thought about putting the bird in the living room, and we decided that we didn't want it there either."

"OK," I said. Then I asked, "Jim, do you have a terrace or balcony in your apartment? Perhaps you have another place to put the bird?"

"No, there is no other place to put the bird," he replied.

Having looked at this situation from every angle, I finally asked, "Jim, have you thought about getting rid of the bird?"

"No," he retorted.

"Well, Jim," I said, "the moral of your clutter-cleaning story is that when you want to make a change, something has got to give. You cannot change and stay the same simultaneously."

Cleaning clutter can forge change in your life, and change usually is an unsettling prospect. The question is whether you want to be unsettled by having clutter or upset by *not* having clutter.

BECOMING A CLUTTER CONNOISSEUR

Like a wine connoisseur who can tell the vintage with a taste, or a "nose" who can break down the ingredients of a perfume with a sniff, you can develop your sensory awareness to clutter by becoming familiar with its different varieties. Acquiring an appreciation for it in all its different forms can be useful when it comes to cleaning it up and preventing it from accumulating again. The following is a glossary of terms to help sharpen your detection devices:

Garbage. In its most basic form, clutter is garbage. On the average, three-quarters of the piles of papers on desks and tabletops are things that just have not yet been tossed. It is nothing more complicated than that.

I had one client who had a row of neatly tied bags on the bottom of one closet each labeled by year. Each bag contained that year's unopened mail. This was the same man whose hallway was lined with boxes piled high to the ceiling. The boxes were emptied in his diligence to clean, but never tossed out so that his new clutter-free identity could shine through.

Remember: throwing out your garbage is part of the process.

A mass of mixed-up, jumbled, unlike objects is clutter. The cat's toys, stockings from Bloomingdale's, unpaid bills and the daily mail, and your car and house keys, all piled on top of the entry-hall table are clutter. The notes from a class, a little jewelry, some makeup, and a collection of loose change emptied out of a purse and put on top of a dresser are clutter.

Clutter is like a run-on sentence. It has no logic. A simple step to develop good reasoning is this: Separate all unrelated items from one another.

Unfinished business is clutter. A scrap of paper with a telephone number of someone whose call you have not yet returned, a letter you have been meaning to respond to, a half-wrapped package earmarked for the post office, bags of clothing standing at attention by the front door ready to be given away, an unreturned catalog purchase, and a long list of undone to-do's—they are clutter as unfinished business.

In the heat of summer when I came across unopened Christmas gifts in one client's clutter, it was too obvious not to ask what they were doing there. "Oh, I keep telling my sister, 'Let's do Christmas,'" my client replied. Not celebrating Christmas by the time July rolls around is definitely unfinished business.

Lots of little unfinished businesses form clusters of clutter that are usually characterized by their mobility. Unfinished business moves from the mantel of the fireplace to the dining room table and then to a bureau in the bedroom, forming a path of destruction until its call for help is answered. If left unattended for too long, clusters of petty unfinished business can turn into big problems, major headaches, and costly mistakes.

Unconfrontable areas of life are clutter. Clutter is like a fungus growing on areas of life that you wish were not there in the first place but that will not disappear, regardless of how far down in the pile they are put. Usually, at the core of such a mess is something you are avoiding, knowingly or unknowingly. It is an area of life you literally want to bury but that, instead of disappearing, burgeons to the point of overwhelming your life.

One of my clients was in the midst of separating from her husband, and the emotional turmoil seeped into her business affairs, throwing her papers, as well as her life, into a state of chaos. Her unwillingness to settle divorce papers, pay taxes, and submit insurance claims all reflected her inability to confront her loss and her life ahead. Unsigned wills and reminders to reserve cemetery plots oftentimes can keep moving from pile to pile.

Clutter increases in direct proportion to the amount of time you ignore a problem. Take action and watch your dread dwindle as your clutter is reduced.

Hanging onto or dishonoring the past is clutter. Photographs and memorabilia are the most common variety of this type of clutter. If photographs are bunched in bags or tossed in with today's mail, they constitute a mess, not a fond memory that can be fully shared or appreciated.

The most striking example that I have seen of this sort of clutter was a man whose home was more of a monument to his past than a breeding ground for the future. His apartment was crammed with everything, from university diplomas to mementos from his fortieth and fiftieth birthday parties, to advertisements from his father's long-defunct business, and to sports trophies and memorabilia dating back to a time when the Dodgers were still in Brooklyn. His whole life was on display, making his apartment a museum of the past, rather than a showcase of his future.

Indecision turns into clutter. "I'm not sure if I will ever wear that again," "I can't decide if I'll attend that event," "It's possible I may start knitting again," "I'm not sure whether to donate to my college or an AIDS charity." Sound familiar?

When you catch yourself being indecisive, it is a warning sign that you are headed down the tunnel toward clutter. When enough unworn clothes collect, invitations amass unanswered, or a long-abandoned knitting project takes up space, you've got clutter.

Clutter is all the things you push aside and think you will decide on later. Usually, before that day comes, moths have eaten the clothes, parties have come and gone, other hobbies dominate your time, and a deluge of other requests for donations complicate the decision of where to contribute. By not making choices, you have chosen to compound clutter.

The fear of regret or of making mistakes often keeps people from tossing out objects or making simple decisions. I once spotted an inspirational saying on the white board hanging at the back of a subway token booth. These words of wisdom broke the agony of one rush hour: "Fear is that little darkroom where negatives are developed." Take a more positive approach to making choices before you push things aside, and watch your confidence grow instead of your clutter.

DISTINGUISHING CLUTTER FROM ORGANIZATION AND BEAUTIFICATION

People often launch into cleaning clutter by buying new shelves, file cabinets, drawer systems, and any one of a zillion organizational doodads on the market today. Their hearts are invariably in the right place and their initiative is worthy of praise, but their actions are premature. Clutter cleaning is related to getting organized and beautifying your space, but it is not the same thing.

Cleaning clutter is a process of assessing all the things in your environment in terms of the practical purposes that they serve. Things that make you feel good, function better, and contribute to the quality of your life in some way can stay; all else goes. Deciding where to put what you are keeping is organizing, and doing it with style is beautification. Organizing overlaps both clutter cleaning and beautification.

For example, a predominant theme in one of my client's (I'll call her Lucy) clutter was shoes. Shoes were everywhere we looked—on the top and bottom of closets, under the bed, tossed across the living room, and on the many shelves that were custom built for them. Lucy had about two hundred pairs of shoes she had collected in various buying frenzies whenever she could find a style for her hard-to-fit foot. If we had bought shoe organizers before we cleaned her shoe clutter, she would have had to buy out the store. However, after gathering all the footwear together and evaluating each pair on the basis of what kind of shape they were in and whether they still fit her feet and her lifestyle, we were left with about fifty pairs of shoes. The decluttering part of Lucy's process was complete. Incorporating the shoes she was left with in a manageable and aesthetic way into her bedroom was the organizational and beautification phase of Lucy's work. Knowing the real number of shoes that she actually was keeping informed Lucy's search for proper storage, as did keeping a picture of her decorating goals in mind.

I want to discourage you from buying organizational apparatus or eliminating any that you already have until after you finish decluttering. Decluttering at the outset of your efforts to bring order to chaos will help you avoid buying what you do not need and make it unnecessary to get rid of what you really can use. In addition, without clutter to obscure your vision, you will see more clearly how to embellish your atmosphere through its decor.

Because organizational solutions to your problems are so plentiful, having an idea of how you want things to look will facilitate your selection. For example, papers will naturally be more organized when you declutter them and set up a filing system. However, whether you install the papers in a filing cabinet that is vertical or lateral; wooden or metal; brown, black, or wicker; stationary or on wheels is a matter of organizing and decorating. To make these kinds of decisions, it is a good idea to wait until you declutter and have a decorating scheme in mind.

If you keep the differences between decluttering, organizing, and beautifying in mind when catalogs arrive in droves in your mailbox, the catalogs can begin to take on a whole new meaning. Instead of their adding to your clutter, you can look at them with an eye to answers to your organizational problems or as a way to meet your decorating desires. Catalogs have many good things to offer that cannot easily be found in retail stores.

Although decluttering, organizing, and beautifying are independent of each other, they are interrelated. And although it is usually better to wait until you are finished decluttering before you move on to organizing and beautifying, there are exceptions. For example, while clutter cleaning Agnes's dining room table, we discovered that this was a place reserved for items foremost on her mind. The items were as randomly placed there as they were being haphazardly handled in her life.

As we cleaned, Agnes aligned what she wanted in her life with the actions she needed to take to get what she wanted. Then as she sorted through the belongings, she had to choose those that were relevant to helping her achieve her goals. This process led to clearing her dining room table. I suggested putting flowers on the table. Flowers were not a choice that she had to live with forever, but they were an immediate way to replace the mess with something more beautiful.

When I returned the following week, red roses were the new centerpiece of the place she always reserved for things of greatest importance to her. I learned that the flowers had come from a suitor. Things that make life a little more lovely are naturally introduced into the space you create when you clean your clutter. Welcome them!

IT'S NICE TO KNOW YOU'RE NOT ALONE

People who arrive on the first day of my clutter cleaning workshops and seminars are usually relieved to discover that they are not the only ones in the class. Before they lift their heads above the clutter they are drowning in, many people are ashamed that they have it, believe there is something wrong with them because they do, and think they are the only ones with the problem.

You do not have to look far from the surface to see that clutter is a burgeoning issue in modern society today. This fact may not make you feel any better at first, but putting things in perspective can help you to be less hard on yourself. The number of people who are coming out of their closets to seek professional help with cleaning their clothes, papers, and paraphernalia is reaching significant-enough proportions to support the rise of a new industry. From its inception in 1985, the National Association of Professional Organizers has increased its membership to 850, with representatives in the United States, Canada, and throughout the world, and it is growing at a rate of 100 members per year.

Magazines, newspapers, and television stations contain numerous articles about how to get organized. One psychologist tried to measure the problem by counting how many Americans are hoarders. Jeff Campbell, author of *Clutter Control* (Dell Publishing, 1992), referred to an article in the February 10, 1990 *San Francisco Examiner* entitled "The Pack-Rat Phenomenon" by R. Lichtenstein, which quoted California State University psychology professor Lynda W. Warren's estimate that at least one person in ten in the United States is a chronic saver. I do not need to go further than my own experience with my business Lighten Up! Free Yourself from Clutter to know that all kinds of people everywhere are eager for ways to cope with this problem. The mere mention that I am a clutter consultant during dinner with a group of strangers starts them telling intimate tales of their dilemmas with clutter. The topic can consume the meal to the point of surprise, and even embarrassment, to me.

In addition to looking at the cluttered conditions in society at large, it is revealing to consider the number of people who are facing various life circumstances that can precipitate clutter. The one million students who graduate from college each year enter a time of tumult when faced with establishing themselves in careers and setting up new lives. At the same time, an average of 35.5 million people who retire from the workforce annually encounter a new need to adjust and restructure. Gearing up for something new or winding down from something old can be disruptive for people who are going through divorce (1.2 million in 1992); becoming first-time parents (1.7 million in 1990); being downsized from jobs, now working from home, or moving from one home or city to another (18 percent of the population did so in 1989); or seeking a mate (42.3 percent of the population over age eighteen is unmarried).

Review any tumultuous situation in your own life that may be resulting in clutter. See if it is a problem that is not only personal but one that many people share. If you use the clutter-cleaning process not only as a way to become neater and tidier, but as a vehicle to address your circumstances so they become more manageable, clutter cleaning will not be a source of shame. It will become an act of courage. Your success with clutter will be your pride and an inspiration to others.

THERE IS NO END TO CLUTTER

I would place bets on the fact that you have come to this book looking for a way to eliminate clutter from your life forever. You may as well know the truth right from the start: There is no end to clutter. It may come as bad news that the mail will keep coming, seasons will keep changing, bills will always make their way to your door, you will go to conventions and fill bags with paper goodies, your climb up the corporate ladder will involve starting and finishing projects one after the next, and you will transition from one phase of life to the next, dragging along or dropping off stuff as you go. As long as you still have blood running through your veins, a stream of objects will keep passing in front of you throughout your life. Clutter is endless. But wait, there is good news.

Along with letting go of the false notion that there is an end to clutter, you can give up the expectation that there is some place for you to get to that does not even exist. Instead of feeling frustrated with clutter, knowing that it never ends can give you a feeling of relief. Understanding the true character of clutter can enable you to reinvent your relationship with it so you are empowered, rather than defeated, by it. You can stop trying to have clutter be something it is not.

Rather than think that one day your clutter will be gone forever, I suggest that you instead try to develop a lifelong relationship with your physical environment that makes it a joyful place in which to dwell.

GROUND ZERO

Although there is no end to clutter, your decluttering journey does have a destination. Instead of aiming to reach the end of clutter, you can be on the lookout for a neutral zone that I call Ground Zero. Ground Zero is like a moving target point or outpost on the clutter-cleaning frontier. Although it is elusive, it is not a mirage; it really exists. Become familiar with it as you change your way with clutter.

You will know that you have arrived at Ground Zero when everything in your physical environment is there because you consciously determined that it would be. It all adds something to your life. When each and every item has been subject to the clutter-cleaning process—all the paperwork, clothes, and things in all areas of your dwelling—and dealt with accordingly, you will know that you have landed at Ground Zero.

Then the character of Ground Zero will change. Ground Zero will still be the focal point of your efforts to clean your clutter, but it will exist in narrower spheres. Your environment will still have clutter here and there from time to time, but the overall quantity of clutter will have been reduced, the time required to clean it will be minimized, your ability to clean it up will have evolved, and Ground Zero will not be virgin soil. The clear surfaces indigenous to Ground Zero will be seen more often.

When you are clutter free, getting to Ground Zero at the end of every week is a good standard.

2

What Are You Making Room For?

You can start to gain new appreciation for how physical objects can work for you, instead of against you, by asking yourself, What am I making room for in my life by cleaning clutter? You most definitely will be clearing space for whatever is on the other side of that mountain of clutter by cleaning it. But what is that? What are you clearing space for?

Many people say that what they want to achieve in cleaning clutter is to feel good and have peace. These are undoubtedly worthy goals, but they are not precise enough. What will make you feel good beyond cleaning clutter, and what will give you peace beyond cleaning clutter? If you say you want to be happy, but have no idea what would put a smile on your face, you will not know where to direct your energies or physical objects to help you get what you want.

Although at one time critical thinking about the meaning of life may have entailed going to the top of a mountain and contemplating for days on end, times have changed. Now you don't have to climb any higher than the pile on your desk or the jam-up in your closet, and all you have to do is take a lunch break at first.

Get a sheet of paper and a pencil and carve out an hour to spend by yourself. Wake up an hour earlier than usual. Turn off the television. Take a personal day off from work. Take your children (if you have them) to your mother's house for a night. Make some effort to take a few minutes to jot down some of your thoughts about how your life would be if you could have it be any way you wanted it to without clutter in the way. Make long- and short-term goals as you look ahead to a new beginning. These goals will help you when it comes time to clean as they will inform you about what to toss and what to keep, how to organize things, and even what you need to buy. Having objectives and strategies for achievement has always been a good business practice. Borrowing this approach to clean clutter will help you implement the process.

People I have worked with have used cleaning clutter to make room to transition to new phases in life, to grow in a business or career, to improve their satisfaction with relationships, to recover from illnesses or addictions, and to heal from trauma, such as the death of a loved one or loss through divorce. They have used cleaning clutter to improve the quality of their lives, as well as to discover how to contribute to others'.

For example, the realization that clutter had crept up on her came to one client when she was home from work long enough to notice it after having knee-replacement surgery. She saw the opportunity to heal more quickly by paying attention to her future, rather than to her pain. We worked at her bedside, and she attributes her swift recovery to cleaning clutter.

Another client tossed trash and refiled all the papers related to a company he sold, so he could pass them along in an orderly fashion to the new owner and thereby make room to restructure his finances so that charitable giving reflected his benevolence. Opening space for his next business venture and unleashing a creative block he felt he had in his personal life were also on his list of objectives for cleaning clutter.

I have worked with authors, artists, and photographers who have sought to open the space for more creativity and a Broadway leading man who wanted to feel as much like a star at home as he did in his backstage dressing room. Many people have used clutter cleaning to help them through the process of divorce, adapt to a new marriage, have more satisfying relationships, or simply make room for more dates.

The answer to the question "What are you making room in your life for by cleaning clutter" is probably not far from the surface. It is likely that what comes to mind first will be enough to get you started. You can always reshape or add to your goals as you clean.

COLLAGE EXERCISE

If you find it easy to decide what you want to make room for in your life by cleaning your clutter, you may want to skip this section and read on. But if you find yourself stuck, this exercise may help you. Or, you can just do it for fun. It can provide a way for you to tap into your heart and reveal your unconscious desires.

Gather an assortment of magazines. (If you've been wondering what to do with that pile of magazines that is collecting dust in the corner, here's your chance!) Flip through the pages and clip anything that attracts your interest on a visceral or intellectual level. You may find yourself clipping photographs, artwork, advertisements, headlines, or random words from the text. As you clip, keep in mind what you want in specific areas of your life, including your family and personal life, your work, and your finances, as well as the quality you want to bring to relationships of all kinds. Or you can just let your selections be random. Usually there are no accidents.

When you have gone through a handful of magazines, spread out your clippings on the floor or table and begin to arrange them on a big poster board or newsprint paper that you can buy at an office supply or stationery store. You can arrange the clippings all on one sheet or on separate sheets according to the categories mentioned in the previous paragraph. How you arrange them on the page is part of the creative process. Glue your clippings down.

One thing that I have found interesting is that some students stop short of pasting down their images on the paper. One student who hesitated to glue down what she had clipped said that she was always great at dreaming, but not good at commitment. It was an interesting thing to notice and a good clutter-cleaning lesson. When one student asked the entire class to rally around her poster because she had not yet glued her images to the paper, I remarked that I was uncertain whether I should advise her to get glued or unglued to make room for what she wanted!

When you are finished with your collage, stand back and take a look at what you see. It will be revealing. You may not understand everything you put down on your collage at first, but time will tell how and why things appeared. One collage I did for myself on what I wanted in my personal life had a line of text that read "Art Becomes You." I had long ago dreamed that I would collect art but had never pursued my interest. Nonetheless, I found it interesting that it had appeared on my poster. About midway through the next year, however, a friend who knew I had not come to a decision about what to hang on my living room wall told me that I should go to an art show that a painter we both knew was having. I called the artist and asked her to visit my house. The fact that she selected a work of art from her archives that was perfect for my apartment gave it special meaning. The collage helped bring to life my latent desire to own art with an added personal touch that I liked.

One student had the insight that she had done the same

thing with her apartment that she had done with her collage. She put things there she thought she should have, even though they were not what she really wanted.

See what insights you have when you do your collage. Do one at the beginning of your clutter-cleaning process and at the start of every year to give direction to your life for the months ahead. If life is moving at a particularly fast clip, make new collages more frequently than just once a year.

Take a mental snapshot of the collage and refer to it whenever you are cleaning your clutter and when life calls on you at any time to act in accordance with your true self.

It is easy to overlook how powerful the collage exercise can be in helping you discover or rediscover your dreams because it seems to be reminiscent of childhood. A return to innocence, however, combined with your worldly experience, is an unbeatable combination that can inspire and guide you as you make room for more, not less, of what you want.

Doing a collage can be one way to define a purpose for cleaning clutter. The following contemplation and visualization exercise can be another.

CONTEMPLATION AND VISUALIZATION EXERCISE

The contemplation and visualization exercise that follows can be used to review your current circumstance objectively, to dream about what you want, and to begin to see yourself taking steps toward where you want to be. Record the words on an audiotape or have someone with a soothing voice do it for you. Then find a quiet place and time to play the tape back while you relax, let your mind go, and allow the words to lead you:

Close your eyes and relax. Take a few moments to let go of the tensions, upsets, and activities of the day. Breathe in thoughts and feelings that you or others around you have that are not loving, caring, and nurturing. Breathe out fresh air and light.

Breathe in thoughts that do not support you and breathe out vibrant and creative thoughts. Good.

Now, visualize approaching your home or apartment and putting the key in the door. Notice what you see as soon as you enter. Just notice what is there without questioning or judging it. If you are wearing a coat, take it off and hang it up.

Now, we are going to take a tour of your house or apartment to bring to the forefront of your conscious mind the way things are now.

You will not be expected to do anything. Just keep washing away any negative feelings that may come up. Let go of any feelings of shame or guilt. Let anxiety and frustration roll off your back. We are not taking a tour to evaluate your worthiness as a human being. We just want to remind you of all your current possessions. You are growing and changing now, and you want to embrace fully the way things are so you can move forward. You cannot move from where you are not. You can only move from where you are; so, we are taking a tour of where you currently reside as a first step toward moving closer to who you are becoming and how you want to live.

Go to the living room and look around. Notice what is on the surface of things, including tables, chairs, other furniture, and floors. Notice any papers, magazines, clothing, and books. Notice the way that it is and have the way it is be OK with you. Good.

Now, open the drawers and cabinets or closets in the living room and let the energy of the past surface and evaporate. Notice what is folded, piled, and filed in every area of the living room and accept how things are now. Good.

Now, move to your bedroom and take a look around. Notice what is where. Move slowly from one end of the room to the other, reviewing how you now live and use this room. Open the closets and see the condition of your clothing. Take a few moments and touch each item you see. If there are bags or boxes there, open them up. Continue on your journey through the bedroom until you are fully reacquainted with what is there.

Next, leave your bedroom and go to the bathroom. Once again, look at everything you have in your bathroom. Open the medicine chest and check all the medicines, remedies, sundries, and toiletries. Notice what you have and what you use. Notice what you touch daily and what you did not even know was there. Notice what is under the sink, on the tub, and on shelves in the bathroom. Stand back and survey the entire room before you move to the kitchen.

OK. Now go to the kitchen and look around. What is on the counters, on top of the refrigerator, and on the shelves? Open all the cabinets and leave everything exposed so you can see everything you have. Accept it all exactly the way it is now.

Go to where you keep your financial papers. If they are not in your home, allow your mind's eye to go where you do keep them. Notice the current condition of all these financial matters. Imagine that your friends or family members needed to reconstruct your financial life or get their hands on important papers. Would it be easy for them to do so? Notice the condition of your bills, taxes, contracts, and insurance papers and the way in which you keep important papers, such as wills, stock certificates, and bank statements. Just notice the way that it is and let any emotions or feelings about it go. Good.

If there are other areas in which you live and work in your home that we have not visited, go to them now and examine with your mind's eye all that you own. Go to the family room, the garage, attic, or basement if you have them and survey what you keep in them. Remember not to judge or assess yourself. Simply notice the way in which you store all your stuff. Notice what you use and what you do not.

Acknowledge that this is how you have lived up to this time. Accept this way of living for what it is and congratulate yourself on being ready to move forward, knowing that you can have your home be exactly as you wish.

Now, go to any window in your home and imagine a huge shed floating outside. Make the shed as large as you need it to be to store all your belongings. It can be four or five garage doors wide if that is how much space you need.

Now imagine opening the garage doors and finding a large, open space fitted with racks and shelves and a stereo with speakers inside to the right. Notice a selection of all types of music. Put on music to set the tone for moving all your belongings from your home to the shed.

If John Philip Sousa's music will help march things out of your home or apartment and into the shed, put that on. If the sound of rock and roll is the beat that will get them from your home to the shed, let it rip. If new age music, classics, Broadway tunes, or big band sounds will set the stage, fine. The choice is yours. Set the mood to celebrate the transition you are making by picking the music to accompany the change.

Next to the stereo, at the entrance of the shed, is a big brown leather easy chair. Feel free to sit in it and relax as you enjoy the music and the unseemly sight of all the things you own taking their places on the shelves in the wide-open shed. It is fine if you prefer to dance at the head of the procession or move around. Just do what is fun for you to do as you watch all your papers, clothes, books, and pots and pans file into the open storage units in the shed. Watch the curtains, carpets, beds, and furniture, including the tables, chairs, sofas, and desks, all enter. Take in the pleasure of the music and the amusement of what you see as everything in your possession files onto shelves and racks. Do not worry about losing anything because everything is placed neatly and labeled by room. It is all retrievable, if that is what you want.

When the last bit of furniture, papers, clothing, toiletries, and cooking and food items have filed in and found a place for themselves on the racks, notice how you feel and what thoughts come up for you. Just notice what is there and let it go. Great.

Now, imagine returning to the empty home or apartment. Before you leave the shed, feel free to change the music. Allow the feelings, thoughts, and sensations of entering empty space encompass you. Breathe in and release. Breathe again and relax. Now visit all the rooms and allow yourself to drift into emptiness.

Lie down on the floor somewhere and spread yourself out. Breathe in and out again and get comfortable with having nothing.

Now imagine how you want to live. Imagine the furnishings and the clothes in your closet. Imagine what you would be doing and how you would be living if your house was just as you want it. Then, begin to fill the empty space with only what is suitable to you now.

Set the mood and create an atmosphere that is conducive to making you feel at home in a new place. Get comfortable with the environment you imagine.

Now rise from the floor, stretch yourself, and return to the shed with all the possessions of your past still neatly stored on shelves and racks.

Imagine three big bins in the middle of the shed. The first is marked "Trash," the second is marked "Give Away" or "Donate," and the third is marked "For Sale."

Go to the stereo and put on whatever music will provide a fitting background as you review all your belongings. You are going to determine what you consciously will select to reenter your home and what you will route to a new location.

Now, call forth all the belongings that formerly came from your living room. Watch them float to the center of the room, hovering over the bins. Next, command those belongings that are relevant to the new you to leave the shed and go back into your home or apartment. Allow them to take an appropriate place in your residence. Those belongings that are no longer relevant to the new you or the way you are going to live will remain above the bins until you designate a route for their final destination in the trash, at a thrift store, with a friend, or at a garage sale. Keep moving to the tempo of the music until all the belongings in your living room are heading in a new and right direction.

Next, command the belongings from your former bedroom to come forth and direct them into one of the bins or toward a return trip to the new home or apartment that you are creating. Each item will parade, in single file, in front of you as you point it to its new and proper place.

When all your past possessions from the bedroom have presented themselves to you for review, call forth the belongings from you bathroom. Notice them move to the rhythm of the music, taking your command. Be deliberate about each item and ask yourself if it is a tool for the future you are building.

When all the belongings from the bathroom have been reviewed, call forth all the items from the kitchen. Take a deep breath in and breathe out. Keep steady and focus on your freedom of choice. Move at the pace that works for you but do not stop.

Now call into the center of the room all your paperwork and have each and every paper file past you for review. Determine if it relates to your new life, and if it doesn't, put it in the trash. Otherwise, let it move out of the shed into files in your new dwelling.

Now that all the things that are tools for your future have returned to your home and all of the things of your past are designated to a new destination, leave the shed and return home. Watch the shed disappear behind you as you enter your new environment. Notice what you brought back with you. Notice what was left behind. And notice what you now need. Notice how you feel. Notice what you are thinking.

Next, we are going to return from this exercise back to the room. Move your hands and feet. Stretch. Begin to hear the sounds outside. When you are ready, open your eyes.

■ ■ ■

Notice what you envisioned. You can replay your contemplation and visualization exercise at different intervals throughout the clutter-cleaning process because what you are able to see may evolve. On a sheet of paper, write down the insights you have had during the exercise. Notice what you kept, what is no longer there, and what you now need.

Take a new sheet of paper and list all the things you will need to do to make what you imagined in this exercise a reality. Then arrange them in the order in which you will execute these actions.

Look at a date book and set aside the time to complete the first task. Now, you are on your way and are ready to refine your plans.

3

Create a Game Plan

Even though you may not have sweat on your brow yet from lifting boxes, burrowing through closets, crawling on your hands and knees through your attic, scouring your basement, hauling stuff back and forth to trash bins, and transporting giveaways to the thrift store, you have already covered a lot of ground on your way to being clutter free. Whether you are reading to get your feet wet before you do any physical labor or are working while you pore over these pages, you've already started to change your attitude and define the new direction you want your life and your stuff to take. You have indeed reached the first new milestone on your way to living in a place where the sun shines, the birds sing, and the cries of Hallelujah! ring from every rooftop for many miles around. Perhaps you have even discovered that there *is* hope.

The steps you have taken are no small feats and will make all the difference between clutter cleaning being merely an extension of good housekeeping and the solution to running a bigger, better rat race or a way to transform your life. So, don't stop now. Begin to take action. Having a game plan can help.

A game plan can be used to support you from the time you start cleaning clutter until you reach Ground Zero. It can begin to give form to your wishes in regard to clutter because it provides the framework for clearly defining a clutter-cleaning goal, scheduling the time in your day to accomplish it, and getting the support you need to stay focused.

TAKING INVENTORY

I once had a health-and-fitness instructor who always suggested that you should examine yourself, nude, in front of a mirror to assess fairly how you wanted to sculpt your body. "Build muscle there, tighten muscle here, reduce inches wherever," she would say. "Turn on the bright lights and look!" she would holler. Although the prospects were frightening at first, given that she was nearly sixty, fit as a fiddle, impeccably groomed, finely tailored, and blessed with a shock of gray hair and effervescence that turned heads as she walked down the street, I figured there must be merit to what she was doing. The same philosophy applies to taking inventory of all your belongings. Come out of the dark and into the light by taking a "clutter tour" of your entire home or office. See what is there that you have not looked at in a long time. Knowing what is out of shape will help you plan a strategy for getting things to be a fit for the new you.

Go from one end of a room to the other, opening all the bags, boxes, drawers, closets, and cabinets. Review what is on top of tables, dressers, end tables, on the floors, and in piles everywhere and make a mental record of what you see. Do not try to fix up anything or clean at this point. Simply survey the territory. Don't leave any area of your dwelling out. Cover the attic, garage, sheds, basements, and other areas that you may not visit regularly, as well as those that you go to frequently.

Taking inventory is a fact-finding mission. It is not an exercise in offering opinions, especially negative ones, of yourself or another opportunity to bemoan your situation. As was mentioned in the contemplation and visualization exercise, do this inventory as if you were a video camera and make visual notes of what is there. Be especially mindful not to judge yourself in this process. Taking inventory is good practice in focusing your attention objectively on what you want to get done and the steps you are going to take to be free of what binds you. It is also an opportunity to give more definition to the big amorphous blob of clutter you commonly may gloss over.

You may discover that things are not as bad as you thought. You may find that there is more work to do than originally expected. You may even begin to find things you had long forgotten.

You may want to take your visual inventory one step further by making notes of what you see and entering them in a journal.

KEEPING A JOURNAL

You can enter written notes of your inventory of your home or office in a journal that you keep from the start to the finish of the clutter-cleaning process. When you reach Ground Zero, you can toss out the journal, along with the last bit of clutter as a ceremonial act. Or you can continue to record your relationship to the physical environment when you want to keep close tabs on your growth in an area.

The notes of your inventory can be a straightforward list of items that you find at various locations throughout your home. Your journal can also be a place to keep your ideas about which areas stand to offer the most if you were to clean them first. If you get stumped in the process of cleaning, you can use the journal to record your thoughts and feelings about what is happening. Writing these things down may help to release your emotions and lift your blocks.

Another way you can use your journal is to take notes on the events occurring simultaneously in other areas of your life during the time you are clutter cleaning. Doing so will heighten your awareness of the relationship between the changes you make in your physical environment and the movement that is occurring elsewhere in your life. It is easy to overlook this relationship, but training yourself to be aware can make you more sensitive to the connection. Clients often casually remark about how they had guests for dinner without realizing that they had not done so for three years before they had cleaned the clutter.

Your journal can be used to record statements about what you are making room for in your life, and it can be the place where you store the copies of your collage. Any insights that come to you during the contemplation and visualization exercise can be entered in the journal.

Another use for your journal is to keep a record of the time-management aspects of your clutter-cleaning process. You can estimate how long it will take to get to Ground Zero and what your strategy to reach your goal will be. Also, you can keep a calendar in your journal that marks your clutter-cleaning schedule and what you accomplish in each clutter-cleaning session. This calendar can serve a useful purpose. If at times it seems as if you are not getting anywhere with your efforts, check the records. You may see that dissatisfaction is just a figment of your imagination and that you have actually taken great strides, or your notes may reveal that you have been sleeping on the job. Either way, you can correct the course of your thinking or your actions by having a look at your journal records.

You may think of other ways a cleaning journal can be useful to you. Even if you keep entering things in your journal and never look at them, just the act of recording them can help you keep clearing your mind as you clean. Without your mind to stop you, clutter cleaning can come more from your true passion.

TAKE PHOTOGRAPHS

Photographic documentation of your clutter-cleaning process is another way to get a true picture of your clutter situation. It is a visual inventory. You can see the volume of clutter at a distance, whereas it is difficult to do so when you are in the middle of it. This visual inventory will help easily identify the hottest spots when pictures of everything are lined up side by side.

Take "before" shots at the outset of cleaning and "after" shots once you reach Ground Zero. You may also want to take photographs at periods during the process and mount them in your journal. It is easy to forget where you started from as you progress.

After I spent a year working with a client to remove the clutter that had amassed in her ten-room apartment, she called me in a panic one day to say that she was back to where she started before she had cleaned her clutter. One small example of the work we had done was to clean her home office. Before we began to clean, the large French doors to her office had not been opened in five years because of the knee-high piles of papers on the floor in front of them. Although it was true that she now could not see past the overflowing in-box on top of her desk, I knew it was unlikely that things had returned to conditions that were as severe as when she started. Yet, she had blocked out the bad memory—which is human nature. This is a fairly simple thing to do, since it is a human survival mechanism to forget. Photographs, however, can help you recall what you would just as soon forget. Reviewing them can help you keep things in perspective and enable you to give yourself credit when credit is due.

Taking photographs of your cluttered areas periodically can help you learn things about the character of clutter. For example, as you clean, there may be times when the clutter seems to be growing instead of disappearing. As you disassemble boxes and bags, unload closets, and tear into piles of papers to sort them out, sometimes things do get messier before they get cleaner. This is a temporary and natural part of the cleaning process, as photographs will reveal.

You may find it interesting to tell the story of your journey through your clutter through pictures. After all, clutter cleaning is just as much of an adventure as any that you may use a travel agent to plan!

Pictures never lie, and a photographic record of your clutter-cleaning process can be a truth-detection device, letting you know when your environment and your vision of how you want it to be are one and the same and when they are not.

GETTING A BIRD'S-EYE VIEW OF THE TIME IT WILL TAKE TO REACH GROUND ZERO

Once you have made a general inspection of the entire territory to be covered during your clutter-cleaning escapades and visual, written, and/or photographic records of the content to be addressed, try to estimate how long you think it is going to take to declutter everything. Will it take you a year, three or six months, or one dedicated Sunday afternoon to satisfy your needs and meet your goals?

If it is too difficult for you to grasp what it will take to declutter every area of your home or office, narrow down your thinking to one room or a particular task and approximate how long you think it will take you to finish cleaning that part. Once you have finished decluttering a smaller area, you can always continue by setting a new goal for the next bite of the whole piece of pie and estimate the time it will take to clean that.

It is not always easy to determine how long it will take to complete each task, even for me. The time it will take depends on a combination of several factors:

- the volume of clutter

- the frequency and consistency of the time devoted to cleaning it

- how often and how long you take breaks

- your power to sustain your interest in cleaning it and to endure the ups and downs of the process

- your depth of determination to produce the results you say you want

- your personal capacity to allow the miracles that result to enter your life.

Still, do the best you can to estimate a time frame in which to meet your target. If you fail to meet your target, you will not have failed at clutter cleaning. You simply will have miscalculated the time it takes to move through everything. Time is merely a way to pinpoint when clutter cleaning will actually occur. Adjust the time frame as necessary.

Linda lived in a four-bedroom ranch home with an attic, a garage, and an outdoor shed that had so much clutter in them that the only place in which she actually lived was the top of her bed and around the kitchen sink. At first, she estimated that it would take three months to declutter everything. I knew from the outset that her intentions were overly ambitious, but a three-month commitment to cleaning was far beyond any that she had ever made in her life, so it was fine with me to make three months the goal at the outset. By the time the third-month mark came, Linda had a greater understanding of what cleaning her clutter entailed. She simply reset the time targets and kept up her efforts.

SCHEDULING CLUTTER-CLEANING SESSIONS

Many people are surprised to learn that they actually have to schedule time to clean clutter. Remember, things cannot change and stay the same at the same time. If you are truly going to transform the condition of clutter in your life and your living environment, you will have to start doing something differently than you have done in the past. Dedicating blocks of time on a regular basis to clean, known as the "clutter-cleaning session," is a fundamental practice that is essential to institute throughout the clutter-cleaning process for an inaugural voyage to Ground Zero.

Setting aside standard appointments with yourself from the start of the process will be an opportunity to exercise a new behavioral muscle that I hope will become a good habit. Since clutter never ends, continuing to reserve concentrated periods during a given week to handle the matters of your life will prevent you from backsliding.

Do not take the fifteen-minutes-here, fifteen-minutes-there approach to cleaning your clutter. Schedule a block of time. I recommend allotting four hours for each session at least once per week for the duration of the time you estimated it would take to complete cleaning. This may seem like a formidable length of time for each session at first. But, cleaning clutter does take time. Once you get over whatever resistance you may have to reserving this amount of precious time to the clutter-cleaning task, you are likely to be surprised at how quickly the time passes. The results you can produce in the period I am suggesting will be visible, though. You will be able to see the difference you have made, which should ultimately encourage you to keep going.

If it is impossible for you to work four hours at a time, adjust the time downward accordingly. But if you cannot rearrange whatever else you are doing to devote a minimum of two hours per session each week to cleaning, it is probably an indication that you are not ready to start your clutter-cleaning process yet. Just like the woman who did not accept the offer to have the magazines she was tormented by taken away from her, if you can do nothing to reserve the minimum amount of time recommended, it may be an indication that it is not your time to start cleaning yet.

Keeping a strict regimen with your clutter-cleaning sessions has long-term benefits. It will test you in ways that are good for your training. For example, you may not be in the mood to clean when the time you set aside comes. But if you wait until the mood strikes you, you may never do it. Also, undoubtedly, more enticing offers will come your way, conflicting with the times you set aside for cleaning. It will not be difficult to be distracted. Just about anything usually seems better than cleaning. The time that you designate to clean should be considered sacred, and honoring it is to honor yourself.

Ending your session on time has great value, too. A word of caution about this point: It is not good to swing too far in the opposite direction from where you began. If you clean as a way to avoid everything else you need and want to do, you will be as unbalanced as before you began this process. Strike a happy medium by working from two to four hours at a time that you schedule at the start of each week, being as punctual about stopping as about starting.

TELL THE WORLD!

One way to make being clutter free more than wishful thinking is to treat it differently from the way you would treat a New Year's resolution. Many people are reticent about sharing their New Year's resolutions with others because they have experienced being unable to keep the promises they have made to themselves and want to spare themselves the embarrassment of failing in front of their friends. Although they may make a valiant effort to get off to a running start with a change they want to introduce in their lives, too often they have forgotten all about it by the end of January. Since making a resolution has undertones of defeat, it may be beneficial to look at your clutter-cleaning process is as if it is a training program.

In much the same way that entering a two-year master's degree program at a university would be something you would want to share with others in your life, letting friends, family members, and even coworkers know about your clutter-cleaning goals will help them to take it as seriously as you do. Their love, support, and encouragement can be meaningful to you when you get stumped, as well.

Other people can make it easier for you to be successful with cleaning and can help you in many ways. If you need child care to keep your clutter-cleaning appointment, welcome their help. When you are unavailable to go to the movies or to dinner, ask them to understand. If you can use an extra set of hands to cart things to the thrift store, set up a garage sale, or move boxes, let them know how important their participation would be. Reaching Ground Zero can be as much a win for them as it is for you, and as it becomes a joy for you, it can bring joy to all.

Just as your journal can be a place to write down discoveries you make during your clutter-cleaning process or to note where you are blocked, talking to other people about what is happening while you clutter clean can be another form of release. They may have observations about what is occurring that can be insightful to you.

In large part, we have been raised in a society in which "making it on your own" is an admirable quality. Toughing it out, keeping a stiff upper lip, and engaging in hard labor have historically been admirable qualities. But part of lightening up is letting go of this idea and including others in the easy, nurturing environment you are creating.

PICK A PLACE TO START

Taking an inventory of your home or office gave you a broad view of your clutter. Picking a place to start is your chance to zero in on where you are going to begin taking the action to clean it. Let logic or intuition be your guide.

The logical place to begin would be the place most closely associated with whatever it is you are making room for. If your goal is to reduce debts and increase income, it would make sense to start clutter cleaning your papers, especially the financial ones. If you aim to reignite more passion in your love life, clutter cleaning the bedroom could stimulate romance. Harmony with all relationships may lead you to declutter your photographs or data-management system first.

When I am working individually with a client, I rely heavily on intuition to pick a place to start. I naturally know by using my senses the best place to begin, and I trust that wherever I am drawn to is exactly the right place to start. Then, I get interested in discovering why that is the case and both my client and I usually find the answer while we are working. You, too, can take the same approach and let your instincts guide you.

Clients frequently ask me whether they should start with the hardest or the easiest spot. I would choose to launch your efforts in the area you think is most difficult. By getting this territory decluttered first, you will not have to live with its dark cloud hanging over your head throughout the entire process. Often what you think is difficult and dread the most turns out to be less fearsome in reality. Everything else will seem like you are going downhill from there.

One of my clients was a man who moved two hundred boxes into his new wife's apartment when they married. Most of the boxes had been sealed since a former move after a divorce. He was terrorized by the boxes and kept saying that he did not want to open them because there were ghosts in them. With a little nudging, I was able to get him agree to open them up. Largely, the boxes contained equipment for woodworking, his favorite hobby. There were no ghosts to be found.

If starting at the most difficult point cripples you, then warm up to it by selecting something simpler. If you are planning to prevail throughout the clutter-cleaning process until you reach Ground Zero, eventually you will declutter everything. Where you begin is not as important as *that* you begin. Choose a place—any spot—and get busy!

CREATING A GAME-PLAN WORKSHEET

The following is a worksheet that you can use as a guide for your clutter-cleaning journal entries. You can use a separate sheet for each item:

What I am making room for: _____

_____

_____

Inventory observations: _____

_____

_____

Clutter hot spots:

_____

_____

Estimate of time it will take to
reach Ground Zero:

_____

_____

Dates and times for clutter cleaning
during the next month:

_____

_____

The place I will start is:

_____

_____

Names of friends, family, and
colleagues in my cheering section:

Getting Started At a Glance

- Just as diets don't work to make a lasting change in your physical fitness, quick clutter-cleaning tips and easy answers alone will not help you manage clutter forever. Transforming your relationship to your physical environment takes time and energy, but it is worth doing because it can make a difference in your life, with those around you, and ultimately in the world.

- Clutter cleaning can be more than being neat and tidy. It can open the space for magic and miracles to come into your life if you appreciate all the ways it can help you grow. During the clutter-cleaning process, you can come to know yourself better, enhance your relationship with others, and discover how to harness the power of physical and spiritual energy.

- Being clear on what you want in your life at the beginning of the clutter-cleaning process helps you choose what to keep and what to toss out while you work. Start by taking an hour to give it some thought. What do you want in your work, personal interests, finances, family, or relationships? As you clean, you can always add to the list or change it.

- Answering the question, "What am I making room in my life for by cleaning clutter?" will put the focus of cleaning your clutter on your future, not your past. Creating a collage (with all those magazines you've been meaning to throw out) that depicts your true heart's desires can help you tap your creativity and imagination. Doing the contemplation and visualization exercise in chapter 2 can also help.

- Once you know what you want, having a plan of action can help you actually achieve it. Your clutter-cleaning game plan begins with taking a nonjudgmental tour of your home to identify clutter hot spots. Keeping a journal during the process, including photographs at the start and finish of cleaning, are other tools you can use to keep you on track. Receiving encouragement from family and friends, setting long- and short-term schedules, and picking a place to start taking action will help you begin.

Part II **LEARNING SKILLS**

4

Principles for Cleaning All Kinds of Clutter

Think about learning new techniques to clean clutter as you would think about learning a foreign language. Once you understand the basic structure of the language and acquire an adequate vocabulary, you can construct sentences that uniquely express what you want to communicate and you can better comprehend what is going on around you. The same goes for clutter cleaning.

Once you grasp the basic principles presented here, you'll have a basis for cleaning all kinds of clutter. Studying my suggestions for applying these principles to the most common forms of clutter, like papers and clothes, will develop your skills. Allow the knowledge you acquire to inform, rather than dictate, your actions. Eventually, you will attain a level of mastery in using the principles of cleaning clutter as a way to clean all kinds of clutter and incorporate who you are into your environment in a meaningful, pleasurable, and peaceful way. In the end, it is best to think independently, so the clutter-cleaning method you use is your own and has your signature style that works for you.

Arianne Phillips, whom the *New York Times* called one of the most influential costume designers of films with contemporary settings, made my point well when she was quoted as saying, "When you are fluent at your work, once you know the foundations of your art, you can improvise."

Regardless of what you are making room for in your life, no matter how large or small the volume of your clutter, in spite of how slowly or quickly you move, you can use these decluttering principles forever to lighten you up and set you free.

PRINCIPLE 1: HANDLE ONE ITEM AT A TIME

The golden rule of clutter cleaning is this: Thou shalt handle only one item at a time. If you look at the project in its entirety, the chances are you will be overwhelmed. With so much to do, it may appear as if getting rid of clutter will consume you for the rest of your life. This feeling will drive you right out of the house and away from taking action.

Try to develop the habit of focusing on one piece of paper, article of clothing, or object at a time. Over time, you will look back in surprise at the amount of ground you have covered, rather than be discouraged by the uncharted territory ahead.

You can't just burn your house down and start over or use a bulldozer to dig out your belongings so you can begin again. The way to the other side of your mountain of clutter is to move through it one item at a time. Every item deserves at least thirty seconds of thoughtful consideration before it is voted either in or out.

The one-item-at-a-time method will help you maintain a clutter-free lifestyle. During a midweek whirlwind of activity or at the end of a seven-day stretch of nonstop comings and goings, you can use the one-item-at-a-time technique to restore order quickly. Later in this section, I explain how this method applies to papers and clothes, the two most common forms of clutter. Once you master the one-item-at-a-time method with papers and clothes, you will be well trained and able to duplicate it with all other types of clutter in any room.

For now, it is important to know that the one-item-at-a-time rule does not imply that you are obliged to handle one item only once. Even though clutter-cleaning lore has long passed down this dictate, as far as I am concerned you can handle an item as many times as you need to until you decide on its final resting place.

PRINCIPLE 2: A PATH FOR EVERYTHING, AND EVERYTHING ON ITS PATH

Another piece of conventional wisdom about cleaning is "a place for everything and everything in its place." My alternate approach is "a path for everything and everything on its path." Keep things flowing in the direction of accomplishing your goals and nourishing your soul.

The principle of a path for everything and everything on its path operates in much the same way as some doctors manage their practices. These doctors often have more than one patient-care room, each called a "lane." Each patient is put in his or her own lane and may first see a nurse, who gives instructions on how to prepare for the doctor's pending appearance. Then the doctor comes, performs his examination, and tells the patient to dress and move along to his office for a chat. After the chat, the patient moves along to the reception desk to pay for the visit or to arrange the next appointment. Each patient is moved along in his or her lane until the visit is complete. You can handle each item in the clutter-cleaning process in the same way until you fully deal with it.

Here are a few examples of how this principle may be applied to the process of cleaning clutter:

I have a particular spot in my apartment where I put things I plan to take with me to the country for the weekend. When I know I want to take a particular file or book or piece of clothing with me, it goes immediately to that place. At the end of the week, I just grab my pile and go. I don't have to think about rounding things up, since everything I need has been in that place all along.

If you are in an upstairs bedroom clutter cleaning and come across something that belongs in the downstairs living room, immediately place it at the head of the stairs. It's now on its way down. Take it with you when you descend.

Perhaps you have papers to copy—one set to mail to a friend or colleague and another to be filed. First, place the papers in a folder marked "Copying." Next, take the papers to the copy shop and make your copies. Then after you file one copy, make a note to the person to whom you are sending the second set. Then, address and stamp the envelope. Follow the trail until the copy is in the mail. Instead of focusing on the tedium of your chores, remember that the routine is keeping you from getting stuck and helping you stay on track.

The trick to being clutter free is to keep your stuff and your life on the same path headed in the same direction. As your life changes, so do your papers, clothes, and other belongings. Rather than stagnating by always keeping things fixed in place, you will be using your clutter as a tool to navigate your course.

PRINCIPLE 3: DON'T COVER YOUR TRACKS

For the duration of your clutter-cleaning process, keep areas that you have already cleared off grounds for more clutter. For example, if you clear a desktop using the one-item-at-a-time approach, think of it as a violation to intrude upon that space. It must, must, must remain clear. If you are in the habit of tossing the daily mail or laundry in the space that you have just clutter cleaned, stop! You can continue being reckless to your heart's content by tossing stuff elsewhere, but not in the place you already cleaned of clutter.

This strict policy serves two purposes. First, refraining from recluttering already cleaned areas will help you keep your cluttered areas clearly defined. Also, by respecting this decluttered space, you will begin to wean yourself from cluttering behavior. Soon enough you will begin to limit the space in which you can clutter. You will literally box yourself into a corner and will have no alternative but to hang up your clothes, file your papers, and deal with any number of small tasks that lead to big problems when left undone. Until you can say you have reached Ground Zero and have reliably integrated clutter cleaning into your lifestyle, consider it an offense to put clutter in already-cleaned areas. Give yourself a demerit and deduct a point off your frequent miracle mileage account when you do! But don't stop, simply correct your course.

One woman I worked with was particularly quick to see the joy to be found in keeping cleaned spaces clutter free. She called these empty areas her "ahh" space. Her objective was to experience more and more of that sense of relief throughout the place she called home.

Another client agreed to waive her right to our clutter-cleaning session (but still pay for it) if she persisted in her chronic random acts of tossing. This is a tough-love tactic that emphasizes the importance I place on developing new conduct. My client accepted this arrangement with a smile on her face and determination in her heart.

The bottom line is this: As you make tracks, do not cover them up again. Keep forging ahead with your cleaning and clearing.

PRINCIPLE 4: LIKE-KIND THINGS, LIKE-KIND ENERGIES TOGETHER

"Like-kind things together" is my clutter-free theme song. What I mean is that by simply putting papers with papers and clothes with clothes, for example, you already have made a quantum leap in your progress.

If you empty your bulging briefcase or tote bag, separate all papers belonging to Project A from Project B, put all the children's homework in one spot, gather all purchase receipts into one pile, and stack all magazines and books together, you have already moved along the path toward decluttering.

Or take a look at your bedside table. Perhaps you see coins, candles, a few rings, matchbooks, reading material, a letter, an unpaid bill, a necklace, and your Sports Walkman all scrambled together. Take a moment to sort items that are similar in nature. Send the unpaid bill to the file cabinet, move the letter to the in-box for a response, and so forth. Gather the like-kind things together first (the rings and necklace), so you will not have to keep jumping up and down and going back and forth as you move things to their proper places. You'll save steps by carrying a group of like-kind things all at once.

Like-kind energies is a corollary to like-kind things. As best you can, given the space you have in your home, surround yourself with things in a room that are conducive to what that room is actually being used for. When you move beyond your clutter-cleaning efforts to decorating a room, the energy of the objects in it will be a part of the aesthetic. Look ahead while you clean clutter and be mindful of the energy of like-kind items when you are deciding where to put them. Choose a place where they eventually will enhance, rather than detract from, the energetic flow of the area.

For example, piles of bills and office papers in the bedroom are usually anything but restful and unlikely to put you in the mood for love. Remove them from this most private and sacred territory.

The daily mail, children's homework and artwork, and the packages of purchases dragged in from your latest shopping extravaganza on the entryway table to your home are generally not welcoming. Why have them there to greet you?

A tool chest is probably better in the garage or even the kitchen than it is in a corner of the living room—not only because it is more convenient but because streamlining energies will enable you to harness their physical and spiritual power.

It is true that clutter cleaning helps us release mental energy that makes us feel better. But decluttering also has a positive impact on the quality of the space. When the great volume of energy contained in all that stuff is shifted and released, spiritual energy is allowed to work its healing wonders.

Like Maechelle Wright Small, author of *Behaving As If the God in All Life Mattered* (Perelandra, 1987), I believe that physical objects retain the emotional energy of what has occurred in a space. Thus, when those objects are released, the emotions absorbed by them are released, too. One way you may identify with this idea is to think back to a time when you were looking for a house or apartment. Can you recall having had an immediate sense of how a place made you feel? If there was a lot of strife in a space, this energy is stuck in objects and can be felt long afterward. Alternatively, when successes and celebrations have transpired in a space, you will feel more positive in it.

I had a client whose clutter sometimes made me nauseous. Because I was otherwise healthy and not allergic to dust, I started wondering what I was reacting to. I began to notice that I felt ill when we were handling letters from my client's mother. The two had a poor relationship, and the energy emitted from the letters seemed to convey the emotional unrest.

Native Americans believe that the positive and negative properties of energy are lodged in the physical surroundings. They perform a ritual known as smudging to clear a place of negative energy. To perform the ritual, they take a bundle of herbs (such as sage and sweetgrass or cedar) light it, and fan it around themselves and then in the four corners of a room. This ritual purifies the energy and restores well-being to its occupants. To a large extent, the clutter-cleaning process helps cleanse old energy in a room. However, when a particularly significant amount of clutter cleaning has taken place, leading to a large shift in a room and its occupants, smudging can be used to help remove any residual conflicting energy. In my opinion, the ritual is as effective as the herbs in making you feel revitalized.

During clutter cleaning, you will be letting go of physical objects that suck energy and close down space because they are irrelevant to your life. In contrast, when physical matter is pertinent to your life, its energy has a generative quality that opens space and makes you feel more alive.

Just as you can clear negative energy in a space by removing things that don't belong there, you can infuse positive energy into your surroundings by bringing good cheer to your clutter-cleaning work. A look at the culture of the Shaker community provides evidence that the quality of the human energy that goes into crafting objects endures in those objects and affects the feeling you will have in that space. The Shakers, who came from England to the United States seeking religious freedom in the late eighteenth century, handcrafted furniture that they sold to afford the freedom to practice their faith. As they worked, they prayed. "Put your hands to work, your heart to God and a blessing will attend you." If you are anything like me, you'll get a sense of serenity just looking at a photograph of Shaker crafted furnishings or by walking into a room filled with things that they built. I believe that Shaker furniture remains so attractive to this day not only because of the high quality of the craftsmanship and the simplicity of the designs, but because the Shaker spirit still abounds in these objects.

Practitioners of *feng shui,* a Chinese system that originated more than four thousand years ago, believe that spirit energy, called *chi* (known as *mana* in Polynesia, *orenda* among Native Americans, *prana* in India, *ruach* in Hebrew, and *barrakaa* in Islamic countries) is allowed to flow more freely through physical space when the objects in that space are not obstructing its flow. This spirit energy, when unrestricted, makes its presence known by producing greater harmony, balance, and well-being for the people who live in a space.

The benefits of clutter cleaning are similar to those of *feng shui* practices. In fact, modern-day *feng shui* consultants advise people to remove clutter as an initial step to allowing the maximum amount of spirit energy to flow through a space. Removing clutter is one of the most important tasks in achieving the benefits promised by *feng shui*. Although the placement of objects within a physical space has a great deal to do with the flow of energy, once the objects are fixed, they need little attention. Clutter does not remain stationary, nor is it fixed. There is a constant ebb and flow of clutter. If clutter is not consistently flushed, it can prevent spirit energy from surfacing.

Pay attention to the interplay of physical, human, and spirit energy as you clean your clutter. Spend some time wondering as you move through your stuff why it is that you can clean your financial files one day and get a call you wanted for new business the next? Why is it that while you are working on a pile of papers, the one that floats to the floor from the middle has particular significance? Why is it that one client removed her office from her bedroom one day and got a proposal of marriage the next? I don't think these incidences are accidental. They are the magic and the miracles that come when you align all the energies in your space.

PRINCIPLE 5: TAKING BREAKS

It is as important to remain alert to what you are doing during your clutter-cleaning session as it is to know when you have reached the limit of your attentiveness. When your mind begins to wander too much, when you begin to suffer from boredom, when you are emotionally drained or physically too tired to continue the two- to four-hour session before it is complete, do not call it quits. Take a break. A break is like a mini-vacation. It helps you to renew your energy and enthusiasm for the task ahead.

Sometimes you don't even need a full break. If you find yourself choked up with emotion that is keeping you from continuing to clutter clean, take a deep breath. This may be enough to calm you down and keep you going. If you need something more, there are two other things to try.

One thing is to stop clutter cleaning and spend ten to fifteen minutes doing an alternative activity to restore your energy. Take a walk around the block, run a quick errand, sit back and drink a beverage, watch a few minutes of the news, or make a quick phone call. One client used to set her alarm clock, retreat to her bedroom, and take a ten-minute catnap in the middle of a session to revitalize herself.

The second thing is to stop working on one clutter-cleaning project and start working on a different one. If you are tiring of papers, put them away and begin work on decluttering things in a garage, attic, or hobby area. It may be the only occasion when cleaning a garage looks like a good idea, so seize the day and do it! A change of activity that still can be considered cleaning clutter may be going to the post office to mail a package, going to the store to buy the gift you have been putting off purchasing, making a phone call that you have been avoiding, or bringing clothes to the thrift store. By settling unfinished business, you free yourself to move forward.

PRINCIPLE 6: LEAVE NO STONE UNTURNED

The no-stone-unturned principle of clutter cleaning means that every item you are living or working with has been put there deliberately and purposefully. Everything in your environment is there with your permission and your permission only. Each item is considered on its own merit and retained consciously for the contribution it makes to you and the future you are building.

This principle also means that when you are going through a stack of paper, you systematically stick with it until you have handled the last piece. When going through a box of miscellaneous items, you shove none aside because you don't know what to do with it. And you overlook no item. This principle implies that you maintain your attention on each detail of the process and that you sustain your efforts overall until the last item disappears, is put on a path, or finds a place.

One client, Gretta, had been widowed three years before we met. She had been trying to pull her life together ever since her husband's death, especially with regard to managing the business aspects of her family's life, her many philanthropic projects, and bonding to her young children. She was making room in her life to start a relationship with a new man. Gretta's closets were as classic as her clothes. Everything in them was so impeccable that I considered overlooking the one shelf holding toiletries, thinking maybe I was being too particular. But I recalled the leave-no-stone-unturned principle and pressed forward to clean it. Gretta climbed up on a ladder so she could reach the shelf and started to bring everything on it down when she suddenly came across a plaque leaning against the rear wall of the shelf. It was a plaque of St. Anthony and on the back these words were inscribed: "Finder of lost objects and good husbands." Its guardianship over her goals would have been missed if we had stopped short of putting the leave-no-stone-unturned principle into practice!

The no-stone-unturned approach encourages you to be thorough. It means seeing things through to their final conclusion. In clutter cleaning, it is the skill that you apply to get to Ground Zero and will be the discipline that enables you to keep returning to Ground Zero daily or weekly to maintain a clutter-free environment and a clutter-free lifestyle. Moreover, it will be the behavior that prevents great quantities of clutter from ever collecting in the first place.

PRINCIPLE 7: DISPOSE WITH SOME CEREMONY

In the process of assessing every item in your environment, you are likely to find many things that no longer fit your life. Although the sole objective of cleaning clutter is not merely to throw everything out, it is likely that some things will get tossed in your cleaning process.

The dictionary gives these definitions of dispose: "to settle a matter finally," "to come to terms" with, "to . . . distribute . . . esp. in an orderly way," and "to deal with conclusively." Because these concepts embody properties that can end clutter as well as dignify life, the disposal of clutter is cause for cele-bration, rather than contempt. Let things go with style and mark the moment with some ceremony.

When you come across items in your clutter that are garbage, throw them away with abandon. Go ahead and tear up things as you bid them good-bye. Sentimental clutter can go with a blessing. If you decide to pass along your clutter to someone else, you may bask for a moment in the joy of giving. Other clutter may have deep-rooted meaning, in which case you can create a ritual around it. One client held a mourning ceremony to transform the energy attached to an object.

We discovered an impeccably ordered shoe box in Mara's clutter, which contained letters from a man whose love she did not return. The letters, carefully and chronologically packed front to back in the box, had been coming for twenty-six years. Mara said she saved them as a reminder that someone in the world thought she was perfect. When I asked why she needed anyone other than herself to know she was perfect, she became interested in tossing the letters. It made sense for her to do so, especially since she was cleaning her clutter to deal with the remains of a messy divorce and to get ready to marry another man. She began to tear up the letters before she threw them out, but I stopped her. I asked her whether the letters were worthy of more tender treatment. With that, she decided to burn the letters to transform their energy. At the end, she said the ceremony was worth fifteen years in therapy.

Whether you decide to rip, toss, give away, bless, or burn, the greatest value of letting go of what no longer has a place in your life is that in some way it sets you free. For this reason alone, dispose with panache!

PRINCIPLE 8: EMPTY SPACE ALWAYS GETS FILLED

When Pandora could not restrain her curiosity to lift the lid of the box that the gods had given to her but forbade her to open, a swarm of evil was unleashed on the world. Such will not be the case for you. You have given yourself permission to dive right into every box, bag, and pile of clutter and to open, sort, and disseminate its contents. The negative forces that had their breeding ground in your boxes will dissipate in the process of cleaning. After their remains have been hauled out of your life in the last big, black garbage bag, there will be lots of empty space and you will be left to bask in the light of what is good for you. But all that empty space can be scary at first.

It is not uncommon to feel some discomfort with the mere idea of empty space (even before you start the cleaning process). Call it fear of the unknown, if you will. But rest assured, as has been said many times before, nature abhors a vacuum. In other words, empty space does not stay empty for long.

To some extent, you can anticipate what will come to fill the empty space because you have already identified what you are making room in your life for. Don't be surprised when you begin to meet many of your goals. One benefit of cleaning clutter is that the most crucial thing to emerge from your clutter-free space is you!

As you make choice after choice about what is and what is not relevant to your life and what does and what does not belong in your environment, the true you will surface. Like a sculptor who liberates the sculpture from a hunk of marble, you will stand in the empty space as vivid as the sunlight instead of a shadow behind a cloud of clutter.

If you are resistant to the notion of revealing yourself to yourself in fear that what you may find will displease you, be inspired by Henry Miller, who wrote the following about living in the grandness of Big Sur, California: "Once there is nothing to improve on in the physical environment one can set about improving upon oneself!"

Once your clutter is gone, you'll have greater freedom to express who you really are, since you'll have a better idea of who you really are. You will be like a tree whose branches can reach for the sun when it has a healthy grip at its roots. You and your home will swell with jubilance when your feet are planted firmly on the floor that was once covered with clothes. As you become more genuine and gain a hold on your life, rather than a clutch on your clutter, you are bound to be more expressive—living consistent with your true desires and communicating with others more authentically.

Some of what shows up in the empty space you create, however, will be unexpected and unpredictable. Trust that what surfaces when you release clutter or that happens to you during the process of cleaning may just be the right thing to move you along your path. There are generally greater synchronicity and serendipity when you and your belongings are streamlined and life's natural forces can flow. When something lands in the middle of the empty space that you create—whether it is a piece of paper floating from the middle of a pile, a particular phone call that comes in, or a "chance" meeting with someone on the street—it may not be an accident at all. It may be the presence of a higher order showing through the clutter to cast a divine energy and a healing power into your space and your life.

If you are feeling experimental, suspend the belief that whatever shows up in your clutter and your life during the clutter-cleaning process is happenstance. Instead, consider that it has presented itself with a higher purpose in mind. If it points you in a direction that you did not have in mind, I suggest two ways that you can respond. You can negotiate based on the direction you would like to go when you are clutter free and clear to know what direction that is. Or you can let go of your doubt and take a leap of faith that you will be led exactly where you need to go. More often than not, this place will be better than you expected.

If empty space does not get filled immediately (with your heart's desire or the unexpected), do everything you can to prevent yourself from rushing to fill it with garbage (clutter) just to take the edge off how uneasy you may feel. Some techniques to deter you include writing about your discomfort (in your journal); telling someone close to you about your restlessness; meditating (the contemplation and visualization exercise in Chapter 2 may help); or just taking long, deep breaths. Be patient because soon enough you will adjust to reveling in the glory of empty space and the perfect thing will come along to fill it.

PRINCIPLE 9: ACKNOWLEDGE THE STEPS THAT YOU TAKE

Many of us are predisposed to being harder on ourselves than anyone else ever is. If this is true for you, it is one behavior that, if reversed, will help motivate you to clean and contribute to your ability to live freely. Regularly praise yourself for the progress you have made in your clutter cleaning—big and small accomplishments. This good practice offers one of the greatest long-term benefits that you can get from cleaning clutter.

Instead of only looking ahead and bemoaning the work you still have to do, take a few minutes at the end of a clutter-cleaning session to look around the area where you have been working and appreciate your efforts. It is common for my clients to greet me at the door by apologizing for not having made any great strides between our sessions, only to then show me photo-file boxes they have purchased, to point out how unwanted clothing has been donated, or to mention offhandedly that they repaired something that was broken. When you overlook your achievements, you cheat nobody but yourself of what you deserve the most.

To help you form a new habit, try listing the things you achieved during a session that moved you in the right direction. What progress did you make in filing? What boxes have you emptied? What surfaces have you cleared? What did you learn? What did you find that was forgotten or buried? What creative ideas were stirred? What feelings did you work through? Where did you get stuck, and how did you get yourself moving again?

If you are keeping a clutter-cleaning journal, include a section for acknowledgments of this nature and refer to it if you ever think you are not getting anywhere or, worse, that you never have gotten anywhere. It is easy to forget that you have earned praise, and your journal can offer a small reminder.

If you are able to congratulate yourself, you may not necessarily need a pat on the back from anyone else. But if it would add to your moment of self-appreciation to have someone else salute your courage or applaud a milestone, then find a family member or friends to share it with or brag about it to. If you need them to say a few admiring words to you, then ask them for this kindness if it is not automatically forthcoming.

SOME SPECIAL ADVICE

The number of people suffering from chronic medical conditions who sought my services was significant enough to prompt me to believe that others like them might find their way to these pages. (In fact, there are 86 million Americans suffering from chronic pain. This amounts to one in three Americans. It has been estimated conservatively that five to ten percent of the population has attention deficit disorder. Some people have suggested that three to six million Americans suffer from fibromyalgia and chronic fatigue.) Chronic conditions such as these may compound clutter, but the benefits to one's well-being in cleaning it and the miracles that are in store when you do are available to everyone. A few special pointers may give you extra help:

- Reduce the length of a clutter-cleaning session and consider putting friends, family members, and/or a professional organizer on a support team for routine maintenance once you reach Ground Zero.

- Pay particularly close attention to the section A Path for Everything, Everything on Its Path in this chapter. During a peak energy period, separate magazines, catalogs, bills, receipts, and paperwork that require any action in separate holding bins, so it will be easy for you to identify what you need to pay attention to first.

- Also, if it will require less energy to set up more general file categories, with fewer subheads or sub-subheads than those suggested in the chapters 5 and 6 on paper processing, this is fine. They will still be more useful to you than having papers scattered.

- Be particularly rigorous about letting go of attitudes and behaviors that can lead to clutter. If you are someone who likes to

clip articles of interest of every kind from
all the publications in print, curb your
appetite and choose only what is
associated directly with what you are
making room for so you do not disperse
your energy more than necessary.

5

Preparing to Process Papers

Regardless of how many lanes are built on the electronic superhighway, I do not foresee a time when paper will be eliminated entirely. I am willing to be proved wrong, but for now, paper is still everywhere. From what everyone tells me, and from what I see, the amount of paper is increasing, not decreasing, in proportion to the growth of the everyday use of the computer. Whether this observation is true, learning to deal with your paper clutter can actually help you develop the skills you will need to keep your computer environment clutter free, too. There is no reason why clutter, particularly paper clutter, has to be an albatross.

Your paper may parade around your home or office in many different forms. It may fill boxes stashed in corners or closets, it may be strewn on floors or spread across countertops, tables, file cabinets, or a desk. It may be bulging out of files not visible to the general public or jamming drawers when you attempt to open them. Yes, papers are insidious creatures, and left to lead a life of their own, they multiply at a rate faster than it seems possible to keep up with.

If you are like many people I have met, you probably think that to be truly clutter free, you shouldn't have any papers. But the fact is, there's no getting away from papers. There are papers you need, papers you want, and papers that you both need and want. So don't deny them, deal with them. Don't categorically reject papers. How would you feel if you were ignored, despised, pushed around, growled at, and tossed aside as if you did not matter? If you were a mistreated piece of paper and had any self-respect, you would fight back and might even multiply just for revenge!

So consider an alternative approach to papers. Learn to treat them better than you do, and you may find that they reciprocate in kind. With a little love, the papers you keep will become the ones that usher you along your path to fulfillment. They will be an asset, not a liability, if you take responsibility for them. They can lead you to greater adventures and pleasures and help you complete projects that you are passionate about, fulfill your family's future, excel in your industry, and more.

Your best strategic position for peace with papers is to get yourself set to file them. Having a home office, file cabinets, supplies, and the right frame of mind will prepare you.

SETTING UP A HOME OFFICE

The first step to peaceful coexistence with papers is to think of setting up a home office area. We take it for granted that a desk and file cabinets are central to operating a business, much of which involves handling the flow of paper. Yet, it is considered to be a revolutionary concept to think of these tools as essential for the home and for managing one's personal business. A well-functioning home office is even more important than the one you have at work, however. It is the command post for your entire life.

Often people will leave their professional attitude at work because by the time they get home, they are too tired to sustain it for private matters. Is it any wonder that they end up with floors carpeted with catalogs; bedspreads of collection notices; and dining room tables draped with sweepstakes entry forms, invitations, and fliers from book clubs? Our personal and work lives are not separate. They are distinct parts of a whole, and both have an administrative aspect.

Ideally, locate your home office in a room of its own. An alternative, is to carve out an area for it in the basement, the corner of a den or living room, a remodeled attic area, or even the kitchen. The choice of last resort is to situate it in your bedroom. Reserve the bedroom strictly for rest, relaxation, and romance, having paper of any kind in it only by special invitation.

If you don't have a computer, think about installing one in your home office. Like cleaning clutter, computers are search, explore, and find tools, and they can help you live and stay free. You can use them to do things faster and to obtain information more easily. If you plan to take technology up on its best offer—to interact and connect with others—computers are worth the expense and time it takes to learn how to use them. Software programs that can help you word process, manage money, keep track of important personal and business contacts, and even plan a vacation and play games facilitate living clutter free. A word of advice for new and veteran hackers: learn how to use the file-management system of your computer. You can duplicate the paper-processing system outlined in this book to make your computer files less cluttered as well.

SELECTING A FILE CABINET

Generally speaking, I recommend that before you buy or eliminate any office furniture or organizing items that you complete the decluttering process first. Once you know what you are actually keeping, you will have a better idea of whether the furniture or organizing items you already have are desirable, both functionally and aesthetically. Waiting to make a decision about whether you are going to sell or keep file cabinets you already own is particularly important because file cabinets are cumbersome and not easy to move. Therefore, do not hastily purchase new file cabinets or eliminate or exchange the ones you already have. With that thought in mind, if you do not already have file cabinets at home, then I suggest that you use cardboard file boxes for interim filing.

Cardboard file boxes are inexpensive and can be recycled and used for other storage purposes once your papers are transferred to a file cabinet, where they will be more permanently situated after the decluttering process. In the meantime, you can set up a filing system in the cardboard file boxes. You will need a minimum of three. Cardboard file boxes are either legal size, letter size, or both, depending on the direction in which you hold them. Unless you have a strong preference for either legal-size or letter-size files and are certain that you will be using a file cabinet that accommodates one or the other size files, buy those that accommodate both.

Once you finish decluttering and know the true volume of papers that you are keeping, you will be ready to select a permanent file cabinet or cabinets. A wide variety of file cabinets are available, including horizontal cabinets, lateral cabinets, metal cabinets in all colors, wooden or wicker cabinets, those that have wheels, and others that are stationary. The most important thing to be mindful of is that lateral files are not as deep as vertical ones.

If you already own file cabinets, it will obviously save you money to work them into your new design scheme. However, do not cling to the ones you have if it means sacrificing what may work best in your new home office environment. You can usually find a buyer for used file cabinets by posting ads in your local newspaper or on community bulletin boards, by offering them at a garage sale, or by selling them to stores that stock used office furniture.

When I operated my own public relations agency in an office outside my home, I had four five-drawer vertical file cabinets. When I decided to move my office into my home, the vertical file cabinets looked like four refrigerators in my living room. Nothing I did—not even angling them in an attempt to make the arrangement more interesting—could refine their look and make them less of an intrusion in my home life. So I sold them and invested in lateral file cabinets that are more fitting for the design of my home.

Regardless of their volume, size, and shape, do not skimp on the quality of the file cabinets you select. Lightweight tin file cabinets are difficult to open and shut and screech when they do, which can make getting in and out of them extremely unappealing and will keep you from staying clutter free. Sturdy, heavyweight file cabinets have drawers that slide in and out easily and silently and hence won't discourage you from managing papers. Also, better-quality file cabinets last for years, so don't hesitate to buy them used if new ones are too expensive for your budget.

Make sure your file cabinets are outfitted for hanging file folders. Most types these days have moldings or hanging bars built into them that usually adjust to fit either letter-size or legal-size files. Older models often require metal file fittings, which you purchase separately and insert in the file drawers.

Take your time selecting a file cabinet to fit your papers and the design of your home office. Take each step of the process in stride, knowing that in the end, your file cabinets will be a major asset to your overall paper-decluttering process.

SHOPPING FOR SUPPLIES

Before you embark on your paper clutter-cleaning adventure, buy the supplies that you will need, so you won't have to interrupt yourself to run out and get them later. Just as you would want all the ingredients before you started to bake a cake, having all your supplies on hand before you start decluttering your papers will make the process go more quickly and smoothly.

There was a time when I would get the urge to cook but never bothered to stock my kitchen because I didn't cook often. As a result, when I'd read a recipe, I'd get what I needed on the spot. If the recipe said I needed an eight-inch baking pan, I would go to the corner store and buy one. (One of the conveniences of living in New York City is that you can find most things you need close to home.) Then I'd come back and work my way through the recipe and find that I needed cream of tartar or some other ingredient, and I'd go to the store and get it. It took a long time to finish a dish.

Then there was a period when I decided to study cooking, and I became more fascinated with the supplies than with how to prepare a meal. I fully stocked my kitchen so that any professional chef could come in and have everything on hand to whip up any dish he or she wanted. In the process, I discovered the desirability of having the necessary ingredients and equipment for cooking in my kitchen. Likewise having your filing supplies ready before you start to file will enable you to whip your files into shape in short order.

Buying supplies is an opportunity to go shopping, and this is probably good news for many of you. It is at least one time in the clutter-cleaning process that you will not have to discard historical behaviors entirely; in fact, they may even come in handy. Here is a shopping list of supplies:

- *Large, sturdy plastic garbage bags.* The object of decluttering is not to throw things away. However, in the process, it is likely that you will, so be prepared. Have a big box of large, sturdy garbage bags on hand. Do not skimp on the quality of the bags you use. A large bag that breaks under pressure will set you back in your clutter-cleaning mission. I'm not generally a designer-label name-dropper, but in this case I will forgo modesty and suggest Glad bags because they will make you happy and Hefty bags to lighten up.

- *Manila file folders.* Standard letter-size, straight-cut, manila-colored folders are my preference. I favor letter-size, even for legal-size hanging folders; but either will work. The cut of the folder (one-third, one-fifth, or straight) does not really matter, but given the choice, I select straight-cut folders. The straight-cut folder has a cleaner line and is easier to locate because the label can be positioned uniformly on every folder. I always opt for manila to minimize visual busyness in a file drawer. If you want to brighten a drawer by using colored folders, I recommend choosing one color. Using one color will preserve the continuity of the look of your files without compromising the flexibility you will have in changing and moving the folders from place to place in your filing system.

- *All-white, "removable" file-folder labels.* Using white labels will again help you visually streamline the interior of a file drawer, and they are more ecological. Buy the kind that peel off when you are done with them, so your folders can be reused.

- *Sticky note paper.* OK, I'll name-drop. Post-It notes are good when used as temporary file-folder labels in the sorting and prefiling phases of cleaning paper clutter. But when you use them on folders even temporarily, secure them with paper clips because they are easily pulled off in the shuffle of papers.

- *Rubber bands.* Buy a medium-size box. You'll use them in the prefiling phase of paper decluttering (see Prefiling, in chapter 6, for more details).

- *Binder clips.* Binder clips come in small, medium, and large sizes, and it's good to have some of each on hand. You'll use them to secure larger bundles of paper that are too thick for paper clips. Binder clips hold papers securely and won't accidentally slip off.

- *Black felt-tipped markers.* Maybe I am a name dropper after all—I like Sharpie fine-point and ultra fine-point pens, and my clients have come to regard them almost as sacred objects. I still hand-letter labels with a black fine-point or ultra fine-point marker because I find it easier to see the names of files at a glance than if the labels are typewritten. Computer-generated labels are superior to hand-lettered ones, so if you've climbed that far up the computer chain, make use of them.

- *Stapler.* As its name implies, the stapler is an essential staple for everyday living, so have one on hand.

- *Scissors.*

- *Tape.* In addition to standard-size cellophane or adhesive tape, you'll need packing tape for boxes and packages.

- *Letter opener.* You can buy a letter opener for under two dollars, but I would urge you to splurge on one you really love, one that expresses your personal style. A grand letter opener will bring flair to the ritual of opening your daily mail. During the paper clutter-cleaning process, you will probably be opening a lot of stale mail. A brand-new letter opener can help lure you to the task.

- *Expandable red-well folders.* Called wallet folders by some companies, these are the reddish paper envelopes that attorneys often use to carry their files. They usually have cloth or rubber-band (preferable) closures that wrap around them. Buy the style that has expandable sides and *no* dividers. You will be using the red-well folders to store prior-year tax papers (see Storage, Resource, and Reference Files in chapter 6 for more on storing tax files).

- *Hanging file folders.* Two things to consider when buying hanging file folders are size and color. Legal-size folders are the most flexible because they hold large and small papers. Gray or standard drab are the colors of choice for the same reason that manila folders are prefer-able—to focus the eye and help your filing flexibility. Again, if you insist on color, stick with one.

Also, check the quality of the brand. The more durable the folder, the longer it will last. Some can be passed down from generation to generation; others will give in after a few years.

- *Colored highlighters or colored plastic tabs for hanging file folders.* You will use these tabs in the final filing stage of decluttering your papers. You can buy colored tabs in individual packages, or you can color-highlight standard white labels to achieve the same goal. (See Final Filing, in chapter 6, for details on labeling.)

- *Clear plastic tabs for hanging file folders.* Although these tabs are included with hanging folders, extras always come in handy.

- *Blank inserts for plastic tabs for hanging file folders.* You may already have an ample supply of clear plastic tabs from previous attempts to create a filing system, but you'll probably need plenty of fresh inserts on hand.

Optional

- *Cardboard file-folder boxes.* These boxes are good for interim filing systems, to transport files when you move, for storing files, or for stashing memorabilia (see Selecting a File Cabinet for more details).

- *Box-bottom hanging file folders.* A box-bottom hanging file folder is like a regular file folder except that it has a cardboard insert to widen its base, to accommodate bulky files, such as insurance booklets, files of petty cash receipts, or letters from family members and friends. You will probably need only a few (six or twelve are usually ample).

- *Metal fittings for hanging file drawers.* These fittings are for file drawers that require metal frames. They are sold separately and are inexpensive but may take some muscle and a second set of hands to assemble.

Add any supplies not mentioned here that you find you need and use frequently and begin to set your own standards for a well-equipped, clutter-free home office.

I FILE THEREFORE I AM

Too often, people relate to their file systems with the old out-of-sight, out-of-mind attitude. Many people leave everything out everywhere, afraid that whatever they put away will be forgotten. The result is an overcrowded, disorderly, disheveled paper condition—otherwise known as clutter! For the soon-to-be clutter free, an attitude adjustment is in order.

Think of your files as an extension and appendage of your mind. They are a place in which to empty your thoughts so you can actually see what is going on in your head. Your files should enable you to see clearly what is important in your life and, moreover, to have access to it. If your mind is like a big pool in which your thoughts swim, a file is fixed and stable. File cabinets are like a net you cast over thoughts and ideas so they do not get away from you. They act as a safe deposit box for what you value.

Once your papers are decluttered and a filing system is set in place, a stranger should be able to visit your home, open your file drawers, and sketch a profile of what your life is about—precisely what is most important to you at that moment in time.

6

Processing Papers

Papers are the most ubiquitous form of clutter and the single best training ground for putting the clutter-cleaning principles into practice. On the other side of the mountains of paper is a valley in which clutter-free gnomes frolic by day and shimmer in the light of enchanted evenings. The gnomes are awaiting your arrival and will herald the moment when, with your head held high, you stride into their village to join them in their glee.

The good news is that the route over the mountain of paper clutter is straightforward. However, it takes patience, endurance, and courage to rise above even the most demanding clutter-cleaning challenges. Start by treating this chapter as if it was an instruction manual for a home appliance. It will walk you through the process.

It is always a good idea to read instruction manuals before you use them or file them away. Unfortunately, many people don't take the time. Whether these manuals are guides to using

the simplest appliances, such as alarm clocks and vacuum
cleaners, or more complicated equipment like fax machines
and VCRs, they give you the lay of the land. You can learn
fully how to use the machines, understand how to operate all
the levers and dials, and take the necessary precautions to
keep them operating in tip-top shape. Do the same with this
chapter: Read and understand the paper-processing method
first, so when it comes time to activate it for yourself, you will
have a good sense of what you are doing.

Essentially, there are three main hubs for paper in a clutter-
free environment—the file cabinet; a data-management system
for names, phone numbers, and addresses; and an in-box. All
three are discussed here.

In constructing a paper-filing system, you will be aiming to
build a structure that parallels that of a term paper outline (similar to the one you learned in fifth grade if you were not too
busy throwing spitballs at the time). There will be several drawers that house main categories of papers, such as financial, personal, and professional papers. Within these categories will be
heads, subheads, and sub-subheads. The heads will be the
labels of your hanging file folders. The subheads will appear on
either the hanging file folders or on manila folders within them
(more on that later). Sub-subheads will also appear on labeled
manila file folders. Here is an example of what someone's personal file drawer (a main category) might begin to look like:

I. Hobbies   *(label on hanging file folder, tab in the center position)*

   A. Crafts   *(label on hanging file folder, tab in the flush-left position)*
     1. Needlepoint   *(manila file folder, labels on front and back flaps)*
     2. Pottery Making   *(manila file folder, labels on front and back flaps)*

   B. Gardening   *(hanging file folder, tab in the flush-left position)*
     1. Class Notes   *(manila file folder, labels on front and back flaps)*

2. Herb Gardening *(manila file folder, labels on front and back flaps)*

Or

II. Beauty *(label on hanging file folder, tab in the center position)*

A. Skin Care *(manila file folder, labels on front and back flaps)*

B. Hair Care *(manila file folder, labels on front and back flaps)*

C. Makeup Tips *(manila file folder, labels on front and back flaps)*

Notice that in the first example, each subhead had its own hanging file and that in the second example, the subheads only had manila file folders. The reason for the difference is based on the volume of papers contained in the files. As a rule of thumb, any time your file grows too voluminous, it is time to subdivide it to make the papers more manageable and to give you greater access to them. When a file grows too large, review the papers to see if there is anything that can be weeded out and discarded. Then exercise the muscles of your mind to determine how to subdivide the pile by applying the like-kind-things-together principle to the task.

Keep your paper-filing system flexible. The notion that once you set up a paper-filing system, you are set for life is false. It is a nice fantasy, but unrealistic and ultimately undesirable. Since your paper-filing system directly corresponds to the life you are leading now and to the one toward which you are headed, as *you* evolve, so will your paper-filing system if it is to remain in alignment with your goals and interests.

What will increase flexibility and make updating as effortless as possible? A hanging file-folder system, neutral-colored hanging and manila file folders, the recommended placement of labels and tabs, and removable labels. You can add files when needed, flush them of garbage annually or semiannually, and change the names or placement of files as needed. With this maintenance system in place, your file system will be a vital resource for staying clutter free.

After you read the paper-processing "manual," put your knowledge to the test by taking the Pop Quiz: Practice with Papers Makes Perfect in chapter 7. This quiz takes you step by step through a fictitious paper-processing exercise and further strengthens your wizardry in setting up your own paper-filing system.

SORTING PAPERS

The first thing to do is to establish a paper-processing center where you can sort papers using the like-kind-things-together method. Any clean work surface, such as a desk, a table, or even a spot on the floor can serve this function. Even if you have to sweep away other forms of clutter to create it, that's fine.

Place three bags or boxes, two large manila envelopes (not folders), and a sturdy trash bag opposite your work surface. These will become holding bins to help you move through the sorting process. Remember, you are sorting at this point, not filing.

With a marker write each of the following words in big, bold letters on separate sticky tags (such as Post-It notes): Financial; Personal; Professional; Names, Numbers, and Addresses; and Immediate Action. Staple or tape the Financial, Personal, and Professional tags each to its own bag or box. Put the last two sticky tags—Names, Numbers, and Addresses and Immediate Action—on each of the two manila envelopes.

Your charge is then to move all the papers from your work surface to one of the receptacles—Trash; Financial; Personal; Professional; Names, Numbers, and Addresses; or Immediate Action.

This is a two-stage method. Only put one small stack of papers on your work surface at a time. The piles should not be so small as to provide no challenge at all or stacked so high that there could be an avalanche. Remember when I said that papers are like soldiers that defend your honor and mission in life? With that image in mind, line up a few small piles next to each other on one side of the work surface as if they were ready to receive their marching orders. Then command one pile at a time to the center of the work surface.

Using the one-item-at-a-time technique, pick up each sheet. You will move through the pile systematically, from top to bottom. Although this technique may sound obvious, many people do everything *but* work systematically. They fan the papers out, dive into the middle, or pull sheets from the bottom. If you catch yourself exhibiting any of these behaviors, stop and correct your course.

Although this methodical approach—from the top of the pile to the bottom—may seem pedestrian, it is one of the most important clutter-cleaning skills, and it will help you develop the muscles to live a clutter-free life. Don't underestimate its importance.

As you move each item across the work surface, spend a moment with it and set a direction for it—toward one of your six receptacles.

Trash is where three-quarters of your papers will fall. Trash is anything that you clearly do not want, need, or use and does nothing to further your goals. If you are uncertain whether something is trash at this point, choose another receptacle.

Financial–business affairs papers include bills to be paid; receipts from utility, telephone and television cable companies; cash receipts; credit-card statements and paid receipts; investment-retirement documents; rent, mortgage, and real estate documents; bank statements; insurance papers; legal documents; tax returns and correspondence with your accountant; statements of frequent-flyer clubs; warranties and equipment-instruction booklets; and important records, such as wills, passports, and certificates of birth, marriage, death, and divorce.

If you run a business from home, add an additional bag or

box marked with the name of your business and the word Financial on it. Keep your business financial papers separate from your personal financial papers.

Personal-project papers are as unique as the individual and reflect your nonfinancial, nonprofessional interests. They may pertain to all sorts of hobbies; background on collections you keep; information on travel and vacations; and cultural and special events. Personal-project papers can include brochures for adult education classes; restaurants reviews; health, beauty, and fitness information; and literature on spiritual pursuits, home decorating, pets, charities, and volunteer or community projects, plus information on anything from child care to romance.

Professional papers are likely to account for some of the papers in your piles. Even if you work elsewhere, you may still have at home your résumé, professional certifications, letters of recommendation, articles on your industry, materials related to professional membership organizations, information about competitors, and background on an upcoming job search. If you run a business from home, you will have even more for this bin, including sales and marketing information, background materials on the development of new products, promotional materials, production information, and on and on, depending on the nature of your work.

Names, addresses, and phone numbers. This is the spot for all those loose business cards, little scraps of paper, ends of envelopes, or names scribbled on napkins that you have been meaning to transfer to your address book or other permanent record. In the first purge, toss them in the large manila envelope labeled Names, Numbers, and Addresses.

Immediate action papers are urgent matters or those requiring some comparatively immediate action, including bills to be paid, letters to answer, lists of phone calls to make, or items to mail. Put these items in the envelope marked Immediate Action.

I had a client whose paper, when teased out from all the

other clutter in her house (a sprawling four-bedroom ranch with a garage and attic) and stacked several layers high in one place, took up the entire floor of one spare bedroom. Following the one-item-at-a-time, top-of-the-pile-to-the-bottom-of-the-pile method, we patiently sorted, prefiled, and filed each paper. It took about three months, one full day a week, to complete the job. My client ended up with three file drawers of material and a memorabilia scrapbook. Her diligence paid off, and she ended up saving a lot of room in her home and in her life for other things. Keep this example in mind if you begin to lose heart.

Despite what you start out with, in the end if you have fewer than three file drawers of papers, you are below the clutter-free average in most in-home offices. But whether you have more or fewer papers than the average, what is important is not so much the volume of papers but their relevance to your goals and interests.

You will not necessarily finish sorting your papers in one session—it's a process and it takes time. Remember to schedule at least two hours for each session, but four hours is really preferable. When you complete each session, pat yourself on the back for the progress you have made—each step you take brings you closer to being clutter free.

When you have finished sorting your papers into the main category bags, boxes, and folders, you will have made the first cut and traveled some distance on the road to clutter freedom. But this is just the first step. You still need to winnow away at these voluminous piles so you can actually retrieve individual items. Let's move on to the next phase.

PREFILING PAPERS

To begin, bring the boxes, bags, or folders marked Financial, Personal, and Professional back to the side of the clean work surface where your stacks of paper soldiers originally started their march. Starting with any of the categories, now begin to reprocess the papers. Let's say you decide to start prefiling with your personal papers. Take a handful of papers from the Personal bag, and just as you did in the sorting phase, reprocess one small stack at a time, one paper at a time, moving from the top of the pile to the bottom. You'll quickly see that the first pass was effective—most of the garbage has been weeded out. This time, as you look at each paper, ask yourself, "What is this?" Then begin forming new, smaller piles, placing like with like.

Keep a stack of sticky tags nearby to label your new piles. For instance, let's say that your first paper is something about makeup tips, and you decide that it forms the beginning of a pile called Health and Beauty. Label it as such. Your next paper may be something on your church group, so form a second pile for Church Group. After you've made several piles (usually six or seven), you'll probably find that the rest of your papers fit comfortably in one of the categories. But if a paper doesn't fit under one of your heads, don't force it—just start a new pile.

Keep putting papers into category piles until about a half hour before the end of your scheduled session. At the end of your session, stop and put each small pile into a manila folder. Paper-clip the sticky tag to the top of the folder, so when you come back for your next prefiling session, you can pick up where you left off. Rubber-band all the folders together and put them back in the original bag or box. At your next session, just continue until each paper is subdivided into a more specific like-kind pile. The papers will still be within their main categories—Personal, Financial, or Professional—but broken down more specifically. Continue the prefiling process until the entire bag is done, with every paper in a folder. Go 100 percent and leave no stone unturned. Then put all the folders back into the bag or box, go on to the next main category, and repeat the process.

Although each person's Personal files will be unique, there are categories that most people use, such as Health and

Beauty, Exercise, Travel, Volunteer Projects, and Hobbies. Many of us have comic strips, quotes, or inspirational magazine articles among our papers, but we don't think of putting them into a file. Why not? If you have these kinds of papers and it makes you happy to refer to them from time to time or you like to copy things for friends, have a file for these items.

Financial files tend to be more straightforward. Most of us have bank statements, purchase receipts, insurance papers, investment and retirement accounts, credit-card bills and information, utility bills, and frequent-flyer mileage statements. Regardless of how cluttered they are, most people keep instruction booklets and warranty information together. If you don't, make a file for them.

If you come across any papers related to a previous year's taxes (such as backup receipts, or the like), put all this material in a pile labeled Past Taxes. Separate these papers by year. But tax-related receipts for the current year can be broken into respective like-kind heads and subheads (such as charitable donations, books, publications, subscriptions, copy services, office supplies, etc.).

Other papers you encounter may include jury-duty notices, legal documents, and vital records (such as birth and death certificates, social security numbers, marriage and divorce papers, living wills, and health care proxies). Put all these papers into like-kind piles and then into manila folders with sticky tags paper-clipped to the front (the paper clips prevent the tags from coming off as folders are shuffled). Rubber-band the folders together, return them to their bag or box, and go on to the next main category. Keep going until all the bags or boxes of papers have been prefiled into manila folders.

After you have finished this round of reprocessing, remove all the folders from one of the main category bags or boxes and spread them out. Look over the folders to see if there are any that could be placed together in like-kind groupings or that are too full of papers and need to be divided into smaller files. Break down these large files and put all the like-kind folders together. Give each group of folders a head that best describes the category. For example, a group of folders labeled Diet, Exercise, Makeup Tips, and Hair could go into a hanging file labeled Health and Beauty. Items, such as transcripts, letters of acknowledgment, performance evaluations, and résumés, could be put into individual manila folders but grouped together under the heading Professional Records. Rubber band all the files in a group and return the folders to the appropriate main-category bag or box.

FINAL FILING

If you have used my method for sorting and prefiling your papers, your final filing will be a matter of deciding on names for files, labeling the files, and placing them in file drawers. When possible, have a separate file drawer for each of the main categories—Financial, Professional, and Personal.

First, label all the manila folders with removable all-white labels. Next, using the bolder of your two black markers, print the labels so you can read them at a glance. Use two labels for each file, placing one on the back flap on the left side and one on the front flap on the right side. The reason for double labeling is that if papers obscure the label on the back flap, you will readily be able to read the label on the front.

The hanging folders provide the more permanent structure and organization for the drawer of the file cabinet. (Use the fine-point black marker to label the plactic tab insert.) The object is to avoid moving hanging file folders into and out of the drawer as you use your files. Instead, you will move the manila folders in and out—that's why I'm such a stickler about labels. With the hanging file folders always in place, you can easily pull out any manila folder from the drawer, know at once what it contains, and see where to return it when you are finished using it.

Insert the label on the hanging file folder that identifies a specific group of files in a plastic tab positioned front and center. This is your main group head (if it helps you, think of it as corresponding to the Roman numeral I in a term paper outline). Next make a second tab for this folder, which lists the name of the first subhead in the grouping to follow the main hanging file folder. Put this tab on the left of the main hanging file folder. As you create files, keep in mind that everything in clutter cleaning is meant to lead you to the next thing. The way you label your files is no different. Placing the tab on the front of the hanging file folder, rather than the rear, leads you into that file. Subsequent hanging file folders related to that group will be alphabetically ordered behind the leader, with the plastic tabs positioned flush left.

The number of files you have will depend on the volume of papers you keep. Under the Health and Beauty head, for example, you may have files for Hair, Makeup, Clothing, and Exercise. If each of these folders contains only a few papers, you can put all four manila folders into the one Health and Beauty hanging folder and still have ready access to all the papers. But if each file contains enough stuff to warrant its own hanging folder, make one for each and put its label on the left-hand side. Line up these hanging folders behind the one with the center tab labeled Health and Beauty.

Remember that the success of your final filing system lies in your ability to exercise the like-kind-things-together principle of clutter cleaning!

When you're done, your files will be invaluable to your clutter-free life. For instance, let's say you receive a letter from your town's beautification committee, which contains the minutes of a recent meeting. After scanning the letter to see if you need to take any immediate action, you open the Personal drawer and let your eye travel down the middle of the drawer until you locate Volunteer Projects. As you scan the subheads in that grouping, you easily spot the one labeled Town Beautification Committee and quickly know where to put that paper. Retrieving it will be just as easy. You can now get into and out of your files in a snap.

At the end of the final filing phase, take a look and see if your files correlate with what you are primarily focusing on in your life. You may find, for example, that you have lots of files on Travel, but you never go anywhere. Maybe you need to reassess whether travel is really a goal—is it your dream to

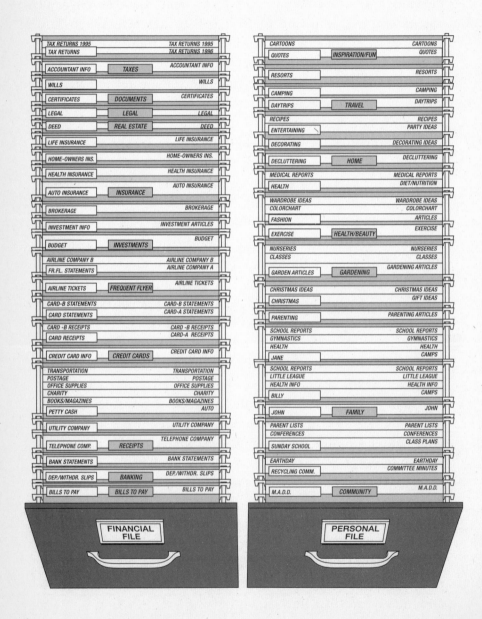

travel or just an idle fantasy? Be honest. If it is a dream, pick a place you really want to go and start to eliminate travel files not related to this place.

I had one client, an avid traveler, who discovered, after decluttering her papers, that she had been to five of the seven continents. She made it her goal to travel to the two continents she had not yet visited.

When your financial papers are all filed, money will be less of a mystery to you because you will be able to see where you really stand. If your bottom line does not match where you want to be, create a game plan of ways you can move in the right direction. If there are projects you are working on to help you achieve your goals, put papers related to them into active files, so you will be ready to go to work. Perhaps your files will show that it is your mind, not your papers, that is hampering your financial progress. Do an inventory of your mental clutter to see if a new attitude may hold the key. If there are papers that will help with your new attitude about money, simply add a file for them and put them in the right spot.

STORAGE, RESOURCE, AND REFERENCE FILES

The papers in the primary Personal, Professional, and Financial drawers of your file cabinet will represent projects, interests, goals, and areas of your life that you are managing day to day. They are, in every sense of the word, "active" files. Once you have completed a project, your interest has waned, and you have achieved a goal, there is no reason for the corresponding papers to remain immediately accessible. However, you may want to refer to these files in the future. So, you are now ready to move on to setting up storage files.

Storage files are like secondary closets (see chapter 8), where you keep seasonal clothes and other items that you do not currently wear. For example, let's say you've been planning a big party (a wedding, an anniversary bash, or the like). Right up

until the big event, all files related to it will be in an active file
in your Personal drawer for ready access. You'll probably have
folders containing guest lists; budgets; and research information
on caterers, music, flowers, photographers, locations, and printers for the invitations. Once the event is over, you'll want to go
through these files to weed out papers you'll never need again
and then move all this material into your storage files. In these
storage files, the papers will be out of your way, but you'll still
have the information to refer to when you plan your next party.

As another example, when planning a trip or vacation, you
will need to keep hotel brochures and information on your
itinerary in an active file. When you come home, move the
material into your storage files.

Job-hunting materials will also go from your active to your
storage files once your search is complete. You may want to
hold onto correspondence with prospective employers (so you
know who you contacted in the past) and other material that
was helpful in your search. It is always useful to remind yourself of some of the steps you took to obtain a position the next
time you want to change jobs. Just remember to flush the file
of garbage first before you place it in the storage file.

If you run a direct-marketing campaign for your home-based
business, you may want to keep copies of the fliers and mailing lists you culled once the campaign is over. These materials
can be kept in storage files.

While you are hunting for a new home, you will probably
want to set up a Real Estate file in your Financial drawer to
house all the associated business transactions. Once that sale
is complete, keep the deed to your house in the Active file,
but move other materials (lists of brokers and attorneys,
information on school districts, and so forth) that you may
want to refer to for a later search into your storage files. Let me
stress once again: Pare down what you've collected to the
essentials before you move the files to storage.

Each year once you've finished your taxes, keep a copy of
your returns for ready reference in a current Financial file

drawer labeled Tax Returns. However, the backup receipts and other papers used for tax preparation can be kept in their original manila folders and simply transferred to an expandable wallet folder (the kind with no dividers will be the roomiest). Next, use an all-white file-folder label to mark the year on the wallet folder. This will help keep these historical records as orderly as current records. It is nearly impossible to re-create your financial history from memory; without the proper records, your worst IRS nightmare could certainly come back to haunt you. The neater your financial records, the less likely it is that you will ever need to refer to them again—this level of organization is a clear sign that you've effectively met your financial obligations.

Place your tax records in the storage file drawers or on a shelf or in a storage box in an out-of-the-way area.

Not all your files will eventually make their way to storage. Often, once a project is over, you can toss the files and move on to whatever is next for you in your life and your work. For most people, one drawer is usually sufficient space for the storage files from all three main file categories—Personal, Professional, and Financial. As you did when you set up your active files, use a hanging file labeled with a plastic tab positioned at the center to mark the beginning of each main category. Again, use manila folders for your subcategories and place a plastic tab in the flush-left position on the hanging file folder to mark the contents.

If you have too many storage files for one drawer, consider buying a used file cabinet to house this information (store it in the basement if you have one). If you are short on space, you will have to be very disciplined about what you keep. Remember to pare things down to accommodate the space in which you are actually living.

Reference files or resource files are the other main categories of files that do not exactly fall into the active file category. They contain the kinds of information that you refer to often enough to want it close enough at hand to gain access to it easily. Not much personal information falls under these categories, but a lot of business information does.

Reference files may contain information on competitors or clients that you are tracking. For example, one client, a human resources consultant, set up a reference file to keep the large information kits from leading organizations in her field. This is also where she kept a list of prospective clients. While it was nice to have these materials orderly and on hand, they did not have to be as nearby as the projects she was currently handling.

Resource files are an expanded version of the data-management system in which you keep names, telephone numbers, and addresses. While your data-management system will contain contact information on suppliers, your resource files are the place for suppliers' brochures, fliers, and information kits. If the resource information is voluminous, break it down into like-kind categories. For example, if you produce a lot of marketing materials for your business and need to find information on graphic designers, illustrators, and printers, place each subcategory in its own hanging file folder (with the label flush left) and place it behind a main hanging file (center label), that is marked Production Material.

If you order premiums or gifts to give to clients for promotional purposes, it may be unwieldy to have all the information on suppliers in one big file. Break the information down into like-kind resources. Your main head will be Premium Suppliers, and your subcategories may include florists, suppliers of printed hats and T-shirts, and suppliers of corporate gifts.

After all your papers find a place in the active, storage, reference and resource areas of your file cabinets, you can return to the manila envelope where you have been stuffing names, numbers, and addresses.

NAMES, NUMBERS, AND ADDRESSES

Using your mind as a data bank for the names, telephone numbers, and addresses of everyone you know or have reason to be in communication with is not only impossible, but a waste of good brain power. You need an effective system for storing this information, and one that is more reliable than your memory.

You can use standard address books, index-card filing systems such as Rolodex, handheld electronic organizers, computer contact-management systems, or any combination of these methods to eliminate the mess of stray business cards and the mass of names and telephone numbers scribbled on the ends of envelopes, napkins, and matchbook covers. And you can finally make sense of all these relationships.

These days, computers offer the most sophisticated method of managing contact information of all kinds, including personal and business data. Once you've loaded the information into your computer, you can also download it into a handheld electronic organizer. These lightweight, portable devices are easy to use and provide a good backup if your main system crashes and the data are lost.

But neither a computer nor an address book will serve you if do not maintain it. Whatever your system, I recommend that you take the time to enter a name, telephone number, and address the very moment you realize that you have a reason to record it. Taking the time up front will save you time later— not just in recording the information, but in remembering the connection itself.

If you are not yet using a computerized or electronic system, consider using your address book only for addresses and telephone numbers of friends and relatives, business contacts, medical or emergency personnel, or other people whose numbers you need to carry with you at all times. Keep this address book in the same place all the time, in your briefcase, purse, or tote, so that even when you are not on the move, you still know where to find it.

Next, I suggest that you buy two Rolodexes, one for more extensive lists of personal contacts and the other for more in-depth business contacts (this is especially important if you run your business from home). Rather than using an A to Z system, consider filing this information by category.

For example, in your personal Rolodex (which is basically your personal data-management system), you might set up main headings (alphabetically) for such categories as Home Maintenance, Travel, Kids' Contacts, Postal Information, Banking, and so forth. Under the Home Maintenance heading, for instance, you'll include the name and telephone number of your locksmith, exterminator, plumber, carpet cleaner, lawn care specialist, and housekeeper.

Under Travel, you'll include airports, airlines, bus lines, railroad services, travel agents, and car services. Kid's Contacts may include the telephone numbers of your children's schools, Little League coaches, Brownie troop leader, best friends and their parents, and so forth. If you do not operate a business from your home, you can keep key business contacts in a section in your personal Rolodex.

Your business Rolodex will be organized in a similar fashion, alphabetically by broad subject category. If as you go through your loose business cards and contact numbers you find that the name, number, and address of a contact is accompanied by a useful brochure, put this material in an appropriate storage, resource, or reference file.

At least once a year, review and update the names, telephone numbers, and addresses. This way, your Rolodex will not be overrun with outdated cards or your address book filled with people or organizations who no longer are relevant in your life. Regardless of what method of storage you use for names, telephone numbers, and addresses, remember that the mindful management of this information relates to the care and handling of relationships.

THE IN-BOX

The beauty of the in-box is obscured by the way it is generally used—as a receptacle for clutter. There is a place for an in-box in a clutter-free environment. But it is not as a container for a ragtag assemblage of garbage, urgent business, to-do lists, and other sundry matters that died on their path to a final resting place. To give your in-box the honor it deserves, use it as a halfway house for actions that may be incomplete but not forgotten.

What belongs in your in-box? Anything that requires an action before it is either tossed or filed, including telephone messages that you haven't yet returned, subscription forms for magazines you intend to renew, applications to be filed, or letters awaiting your response. Be especially careful with invitations that require responses—you can put them in the in-box as long as you intend to respond in a timely fashion. Remember, your in-box should not be a forum for your indecision; instead the items placed there are a three-dimensional reminder to take action!

Make a sincere effort to empty your in-box by the end of each week (Ground Zero territory) and before the start of another. Use the same method you've used for decluttering all other items of paper—one item at a time, from the top of the pile to the bottom. Handle each item one at a time, and when you're done with it, toss the paper in the trash or file it in its designated place. Take painstaking measures to scrape the bottom of the in-box clean, even if it means listening to Muzak while you wait on the phone to see a transaction through to the end.

The little bit of empty space you create when nothing is left in the in-box can give you a large sense of accomplishment. An in-box that is void of paper holds the thrill of another miracle and offers the promise of new things to come. The faster you move things out, the more quickly good things of another sort can enter.

7

Pop Quiz: Practice with Papers Makes Perfect

Just for fun, play around with the following exercise. For the second part of the exercise, you'll need to skip ahead to chapter 13, Using Time Wisely, to help you along. Create a filing system for the papers of a fellow clutterer, Clutter Bug.

Clutter Bug lives with her husband and children. She is interested in spending more time with the family and deepening her practice of yoga. Clutter Bug currently works in the marketing department of a large corporation, and her goal is to save and invest ten percent of her annual earnings after basic expenses. She will have a hard time achieving her goal unless she can increase her earnings by $1,000 per month by the end of the year. She is considering either trying to get a promotion at work, finding a new job that pays more, or becoming an entrepreneur and starting a business. She intends to improve her professional skills so she can raise her fee for services in the open marketplace.

Do an outline that represents how you would structure the filing system for Clutter Bug's papers. You'll be using hanging file folders, tabs, and manila folders. Outline the goals and game plan for each file category, beware of garbage, and indicate what goes into the in-box and address book or data-management system. Specify how you'd use the files and where you would position the tabs. Then imagine what miracles Clutter Bug is likely to experience on the other side of the mountain of clutter.

After doing the exercise (and reading chapter 13) make up a schedule for Clutter Bug based on the goals and interests just mentioned. Take two sheets of paper and divide them into seven columns representing each day of the week for a two-week period. Imagine what Clutter Bug would be doing each day to meet these goals and interests.

Here are the contents of Clutter Bug's paper clutter:

> an article from a Sunday newspaper about day trips for families
>
> a birthday card that requires a response
>
> an invitation to a special retreat with the yoga master
>
> receipts for gifts purchased for business advisers
>
> a notice from an electronic list broker on services for creating direct mail marketing programs
>
> a scrap of paper with a lead for a job
>
> a subscription offer for *Moneyline Investment Newsletter*
>
> an IRA account statement
>
> copies of an old résumé
>
> bank deposit slips
>
> a telephone message for a call already returned, with the telephone number already in the address book

a receipt for fax paper

a draft of a new résumé

a mailing from a brokerage firm about on-line banking services

a receipt from the post office for the purchase of stamps

a thank-you letter from a satisfied client

a handout from a course on how to write résumés

a certificate of deposit

a brochure from the local zoo

a monthly bank statement

a catalog from a book club for small-business owners

a reminder to herself to call the community theater about
volunteering

a schedule for yoga classes

a recipe for a birthday cake

a checkbook

an article from the *Yoga Journal* about exercise positions

an internet article about how to apportion investments

a directory of members of the City Marketing Club

a receipt from a copy shop

notes from a continuing education course on team building

a bibliography of recommended readings picked up at the yoga
center

an article on the best start-up businesses

a mailing about safaris in Africa on which she has no plans to go

a copy of *City Magazine* with a cover blurb about a kite-flying club a schedule of the City Marketing Club's monthly power breakfasts

a payment stub for a magazine subscription

a flier on making your own Halloween costumes

a letter from a financial planner confirming next week's meeting

a receipt from lunch with a friend who owns her own business

a letter from the mayor about the city's on-line services, including cultural events

a stack of business cards picked up at a power breakfast at the City Marketing Club

a napkin with a telephone number of someone whose call needs to be returned

a receipt for a taxi ride to the airport

an offer for a month's free subscription to a magazine for people living in Transylvania (Clutter Bug lives in Intervania)

a booklet on venture capitalists picked up at the City Marketing Club

SORTING THE PAPERS

Here is how Clutter Bug's papers could be sorted into main categories:

Financial items teased out of the pile:

receipts for gifts purchased for business advisers

an IRA account statement

bank deposit slips

a receipt for fax paper

a mailing from a brokerage firm about on-line banking services

a receipt from the post office for the purchase of stamps

a certificate of deposit

a monthly bank statement

a checkbook

an Internet article about how to apportion investments

a receipt from a copy shop

a letter from a financial planner confirming next week's meeting

a receipt from lunch with a friend who owns her own business

a receipt for a taxi ride to the airport

Professional items from the pile:

a notice from an electronic list broker about creating direct mail
  marketing programs

a scrap of paper with lead for a job

brochures picked up at a convention for home-based businesses

copies of an old résumé

a draft of a new résumé

a thank-you letter from a satisfied client

a handout from a course on how to write résumés

a catalog from a book club for small-business owners

a directory of members of the City Marketing Club

notes from a continuing education course on team building

an article on the best start-up businesses

a schedule of monthly power breakfasts at the City Marketing Club

a booklet on venture capitalists picked up at the City Marketing Club

Personal items found in the pile:

an article from a Sunday newspaper about day trips for families

an invitation to a special retreat with the yoga master

a brochure from the local zoo

a reminder to herself to call the community theater about
  volunteering

a schedule of yoga classes

a recipe for a birthday cake

an article from the *Yoga Journal* about exercise positions

a bibliography of recommended readings

a copy of *City Magazine* with cover blurb about a kite-flying club

a flyer on making your own Halloween costumes

a letter from the mayor about the city's on-line services, including cultural events

Address book–data-management items:

a stack of business cards picked up at a power breakfast at the City Marketing Club

In-box items:

a napkin with a telephone number of someone whose call needs to be returned

a subscription offer for *Moneyline Investment* newsletter

a birthday card that requires a response

Garbage:

a telephone message for a call already returned, with the telephone number already in address book

a mailing about safaris in Africa on which she has no plans to go.

an offer of a month's free subscription to a magazine for people living in Transylvania

PREFILING THE PAPERS

Here is how Clutter Bug's papers would be prefiled:

Like-kind financial papers grouped together:

Banking:

a monthly bank statement

bank deposit slips

a checkbook

<u>Investments:</u>

> an IRA account statement
>
> a mailing from a brokerage firm about on-line banking services
>
> an internet article about how to apportion investments
>
> a certificate of deposit
>
> a letter from a financial planner confirming next week's
> appointment

<u>Receipts:</u>

> receipts for gifts purchased for business advisers
>
> a receipt for fax paper
>
> a receipt from the post office for the purchase of stamps
>
> a receipt from the copy shop
>
> a receipt from lunch with a friend who owns her own business
>
> a receipt for a taxi ride to the airport
>
> a payment stub for a magazine subscription

Like-kind professional papers grouped together according to goals and interests:

<u>Find a new job or get a promotion:</u>

> a scrap of paper with a lead for a job
>
> copies of an old résumé
>
> a draft of a new résumé
>
> a thank-you letter from a satisfied client
>
> a handout from a course on how to write résumés

<u>Start New Business:</u>

> brochures picked up at a convention for home-based businesses
>
> a catalog from a book club for small-business owners
>
> an article on the best start-up businesses
>
> a booklet on venture capitalists picked up at the City Marketing
> Club

Improve professional skills:

a notice from an electronic list broker on creating direct mail
marketing programs
a directory of members of the City Marketing Club
notes from a continuing education course on team building
a schedule of monthly power breakfasts at the City Marketing
Club

Like-kind personal items grouped according to their relevance to goals and interests:

Family:

an article from a Sunday newspaper about day trips for families
a brochure from the local zoo
a note to herself to call the community theater to volunteer
a recipe for a birthday cake
a copy of *City Magazine* with cover blurb about a kite-flying club
a flier on making your own Halloween costumes
a letter from the mayor about the city's on-line services,
including cultural events

Yoga:

an invitation to a special retreat with the yoga master
a schedule of yoga classes
an article from the *Yoga Journal* about exercise positions
a bibliography of recommended readings picked up at the yoga
center

FINAL FILING

Clutter Bug's papers could be final filed as follows.

First let's reassess Clutter Bug's goals. Her primary goal, what she's making room for, is to have 10 percent of her earnings available for investment and retirement purposes after her basic expenses are paid. Her game plan for achieving this goal is to get a promotion or research finding a higher-paying job or starting a new business.

I. Financial   *(File drawer 1)*

Making room for: Having ten percent of earnings available for investment and retirement purposes after basic expenses are paid

Game plan: Get a promotion, research finding a higher-paying job, or starting a new business

A. Banking   (Hanging file folder, center tab)
    1. MoneyBags Bank   *(Hanging file folder, left tab)*
      a. Monthly statements   *(Manila folder)*
      b. Deposit and withdrawal slips   *(Manila folder)*

B. Receipts   *(Hanging file folder, center tab)*
      a. Automobile
      b. Books, publications, tapes
      c. Copy services
      d. Gifts
      e. Meals (business)
      f. Office supplies
      g. Postage
      h. Transportation   *(All manila folders. Individual hanging folders are not necessary because the volume in each file is slim)*

C. Investments   *(Hanging file folder, center tab)*
    1. General information (includes the mailing from the brokerage firm about on-line banking services and an article from the Internet on how to apportion investments)   *(Hanging file folder, left tab)*
    (Manila folder. No need for separate hanging folders for each item)

2. ABC Brokerage Firm   *(Hanging file folder, left tab)*
   a. IRA account statement   *(Manila folder)*
   b. Certificate of deposit   *(Manila folder)*
3. Financial Planning   *(Hanging file folder, left tab)*
   a. A letter from a financial planner confirming next week's appointment   *(Manila folder)*

II. Professional   (File Drawer 2)

Making room for: Increase in income of $1,000 per month by the end of the year

Game plan: Get a promotion or find a higher-paying job, research starting own business, and increase marketplace value through professional training and accruing credentials

A. New Job/Promotion   *(Hanging folder, center tab)*
   1. Résumé   *(Hanging folder left tab)*
     a. Résumé-writing tips   *(Manila folder)*
     b. Past résumés   *(Manila folder)*
     c. Recent résumés   *(Manila folder)*

B. Starting own business   *(Hanging folder, center tab)*
   1. Articles on entrepreneurs   *(Hanging folder, left tab)*
   2. Business books to buy   *(Hanging folder, left tab)*

C. Skill building   *(Hanging folder, center tab)*
   1. Networking   *(Hanging folder, left tab)*
     a. City Marketing Club   *(Manila folder)*   (event calendars and the membership directory included in the manila folder)
   2. Continuing education   *(Hanging folder, left tab)*
     a. Notes for a new course on technology   *(Manila folder)*
     b. Notes for a course on team building   *(Manila folder)*

III. Personal   *(File drawer 3)*

Making room for: Spending time with the family, deepening knowledge and practice of yoga

Game plan: Plan special family outings once a month, go to a yoga class once a week, and read more books on yoga throughout the year

A. Family   *(Hanging file folder, center tab)*
   1. Places to go   *(Hanging file folder, left tab)*   (One manila folder contains all related items because the volume is not large enough to warrant individual files)
      (Includes the newspaper article on family day trips, the brochure on the local zoo, and the mayor's letter on the city's on-line services, including cultural events)
   2. Things to do   *(Hanging file folder, left tab)*   (One manila folder holds information on the community theater because it could be done as a family project, as could baking birthday cakes, joining the kite-flying club, and making Halloween costumes)

B. Yoga   *(Hanging file folder, center tab)*
   1. Classes-retreats   *(Hanging file folder, left tab)*
   2. Reading   *(Hanging file folder, left tab)*
   3. Exercises   *(Hanging file folder, left tab)*

CLUTTER BUGS MIRACLES: Let your imagination run wild!

8

Clothing Clutter

While the contents of your file cabinets reflect the most important things on your mind, the contents of your closets, drawers, and shelves—your clothing—should mirror the most important things that you do, as well as define and express who you are. Clothing that is not coordinated with these purposes is clothing that should find another home.

When you open your closets or drawers, your goal is to get dressed, not to get upset. Yet, every day many of us discover that we have plenty of what we do not need—nothing looks right, nothing is ironed, all our best shirts are missing buttons, or our skirt hems are hanging, and so forth.

If the state of your drawers or closets turns an otherwise glorious day into a nightmare, then it is time to do some streamlining. Streamline your clothing so the act of getting out of the door in the morning, going out for an evening, or taking off for a trip is effortless. Although this concept may sound simple, it requires some effort, just as a ballet dancer's seemingly effort-less movements belie years of dedication and practice. The good news is that clutter-free closets won't take years of sacri-fice to achieve, just a few relatively simple measures.

Often people hang on to clothes just because they recall the hard-earned money they spent on them. Unfortunately, even expensive clothing stains, gets worn out, fades, no longer fits (I like to think that it grows smaller), or outlives its usefulness.

The clothing-decluttering process starts with using a few guidelines to evaluate all your clothes. It also helps to develop a fashion philosophy and use thoughtful shopping practices, which means only buying what you really need and sticking to your guidelines no matter how discounted an item is. This practice will save you money and time in the long run—not to mention frequent repeats of the decluttering process.

HANGING ON TO HANGERS

Three-quarters of most people's closets are filled with empty hangers, which makes it difficult to see the clothes that are really there. Check to see if this is true for you and then take your first step in the decluttering process by removing all the empty hangers. It is astounding how much space empty hang-ers occupy. Watch the space open up immediately when they are gone.

Regardless of whether you shop in small haute couture clothing boutiques, department stores, or mass-market and dis-count chains, clothes are pricey. They should be well cared for, starting with good-looking hangers that are pleasing to the eye, yet unobtrusive. I recommend moving in the direction of uniformity in the style of all the hangers you use. In the same way that multicolored file folders in your file cabinets distract you from finding what you need immediately, a panoply of hanger styles and colors can prevent you from focusing on the clothes themselves. They make a closet "busy" and "noisy," a characteristic of clutter that you will want to subdue in your cleaning process. Going into your closet may be your one chance during the day to be calm. Do not miss the opportunity for any moment of peace!

Wire hangers are the least attractive choice so if you can, steer away from them. Return the bundles you may have to your local dry cleaning establishment. Reuse plastic, aluminum, cushioned, or wooden hangers.

My favorite type of hanger for most clothes, including coats, is an anodized solid aluminum hanger. Because these hangers are thin, they maximize space, but they are sturdy. Sold through mail-order catalogs like Kitchen and Home (1–800–414–5544), they are available in gold or silver, which are neutral so you probably won't grow tired of looking at them. Although they aren't cheap, they are a worthwhile investment. Use better-quality hangers such as these for your everyday clothes closet and less expensive varieties for storage clothing. It is also a good idea to select skirt hangers of a uniform style.

To prevent a buildup of hangers in your closet, each time you take something out of the closet, place the empty hanger to the far left or far right of the closet. When you want to reclaim the hanger, you will know exactly where to find it.

Without a mishmash of hangers in the way, you can see your clothes clearly. It is now time to determine which articles of clothing are keepers and which are not.

PUTTING YOUR CLOTHES TO THE TEST

You are now ready to evaluate your clothes one item at a time to determine what is a suitable wardrobe for the life your are really leading and the one you are building.

Before you begin to weed through all the apparel piled on chairs, crammed in the closets, and strewn across the bed or on the floor on the hunt for the wardrobe that would put more of your attention on what you are doing than what you are wearing, sit down and take a few minutes to consider the direction you are headed in.

Try making a list of all your daily or regular activities. Are you an executive? A mom or dad? A theatergoer? A sports enthusiast? A single person who dates often or would like to? Perhaps you are a frequent traveler or a handyman. Or maybe you have hobbies that call for particular attire. Do you wear uniforms to work? You need to have the clothing appropriate to all the things you do. This statement may sound obvious, but how often have you gone to your closet and groaned, "I don't have a thing to wear!" For many, closets and drawers are not filled with clothes that are ready to rise to every occasion.

Nancy, one of my clients, had saved enough money to take a sabbatical from her corporate position long enough to rethink her career. By the time we met, she was spending most of her days leisurely going to the health club and lunching with friends, unwinding from years of stress in the workplace. But her closets were still filled with three-piece suits! Her work-out gear was bunched in a corner, and she had few casual skirts or slacks for an afternoon lunch. She did not argue when I suggested that a shopping spree was necessary to coordinate her clothing with her new lifestyle. Having the right clothes in your closet for the things you are really doing is one way to reinforce your focus on whatever that is.

Next, think about the activities that you want to engage in, but are not. As you move through your closet, you can keep an eye out for clothes that are appropriate for those activities. Buy the garments to motivate you. If you love the opera and still love the idea of using it as an occasion to wear formal attire, buy a dressy outfit and the opera will follow. If it has been so long since you have been to the gym that your work-out gear no longer fits, spark up your drawers with some new exercise apparel to help get you started again. Want more romantic evenings? Put yourself in the mood by having the right clothing to entice you. You can even inspire your clutter cleaning by having ready some loose, comfortable clothes (leggings make it easy to bend) that are easy to move around in. Elastic bands, barrettes, or scrunchies to pull back your hair come in handy, too.

Once you nail down the truth about the way you are actually spending your time and are able to envision new days ahead, you'll be ready to assess your clothing, as you did your papers, piece by piece.

Next, determine if each item fits the size of the body that you *really* have. Clutter cleaning is a truth-telling process, and there is no more brutal test of your honesty than in the correct answer to the question: Does this item fit? If it is too small and you will never be a size 2 again, begin a pile for giveaways. If it is too small, but minor adjustments will make it comfortable, then start a pile of things to be tailored. If it is too large, do the same. If it does not fit, large or small, but you are not ready to let it go, start another pile to be joined by other such items. I call that pile the fat clothes, skinny clothes pile (I'll talk about this pile in the next section of this chapter).

If something fits, but needs cleaning, mending, or pressing, then start a pile for those clothes, making sure that you deal with them appropriately before they are placed permanently in the closet.

Next, ask yourself if each item is appropriate for the current season. If it is and it passes all the other criteria, then into the closet it can go. If it is for another season and passes inspection on all other counts, put it on a path to a secondary closet. I discuss primary and secondary closets in the next section of this chapter in more detail.

Is the item in fashion, or does it match your personal style at this point? I'm not suggesting that you have to be a trend follower or a trendsetter to have a wardrobe that works, but to some degree you will be influenced by current styles when it comes to what you will and will not wear. Assess each item accordingly. Sometimes all it takes to update an item is a simple hem adjustment. In other cases, an item is from an era that has come and gone and you are unlikely to wear it again. You are not obliged to stay stuck in time.

Some people change their mood or lifestyle from one year to the next. They need serious clothes one season, but more playful clothes the same time the following year. If you are assessing your wardrobe while in a playful frame of mind, step back and ask yourself if you can rework serious items by toning them down with different tops, shoes, or other accessories to reflect your current style better. If you cannot, then decide if it is something you are likely to revisit when your mood swings back. If you will wear it at another time, put it in the same pile as the alternate-season clothing. If not, bid it good-bye and put it in the giveaway pile.

If a garment passes all the other tests—it fits, it is in season; is mended, cleaned, and pressed; and is in fashion or fits your personal style—still, ask yourself again if you will actually wear it. Sometimes, for whatever reason, you and the item never jived. Fashion faux pas are all too common. If this item signifies such an error, do not remind yourself of your faults every time you go to your closet by having to confront it.

Once you have put an item to the test and have decided that it is appropriate for an activity you currently are or want to be engaged in; fits; is mended, cleaned, and pressed; is in season; is a style that fits the times in which we live and your mood; and you will wear it, then it has earned a place in your closet or drawer. If it does not, set it on the proper path.

A final thing to keep in mind as you put all your clothing to the decluttering test is your actual space. Part of the decluttering process is learning to live appropriately in the space you are actually living in, not the space you someday may have. If you have lots of closets and storage space, you have slightly more liberty to keep questionable items or alternate-size clothing than those who have less space. Just monitor yourself and do not be mischievous.

FAT CLOTHES, SKINNY CLOTHES, AND THE PRIMARY AND SECONDARY CLOSETS

Your primary closet is the one you use every day when you are getting dressed. Clothing that is not in season but that would otherwise pass "the test" is the first category that should be routed to what I call a secondary closet. I use the term *secondary closet* loosely. If you have only one closet, the secondary closet will either be a storage area or one side of your closet.

Another category of clothing for the secondary closet is evening wear (because it is less frequently worn than casual or business attire), special Halloween costumes, memorabilia (clothing such as the dress you wore to your high school prom or the baseball uniform for your first Little League game). Memorabilia clothes can be kept in limited quantities in secondary closets.

In addition, if you have room in your secondary closets, you are free to hang on to a few fat or skinny clothes. Skinny clothes are the ones you commonly keep in hopes of fitting into them as soon as you shave off a few pounds. Fat clothes are a backup for the times you are in your chocolate phase. On one dash through Grand Central Station, I spotted a woman fumbling with a box labeled "Skinny Clothes." I could not tell in the rush of things if she was coming or going. For many of us, it is reassuring to know that most people have this category of clothing in their closets. When it comes to the fat clothes–skinny clothes phenomenon, discretion is advised. If you are never going to squeeze into that little brown skirt again, you have to 'fess up to this fact. You get some extra points on the clothing-decluttering frequent miracle–mileage plan for this sort of letting go. The discipline you develop in the clutter-cleaning process may carry over to your eating regimen.

I recommend that the clothes in your secondary closet be as clean, pressed, mended, and ready to wear as those in your primary closet. Here's a clutter-free pop quiz: If you suddenly had to jet off to a city with a completely different climate, could you be packed and ready with the proper clothes within an hour?

When all your clothing has been put to the test one item at a time and routed to a primary closet or a secondary closet, reanalyze how your closet is working by using the like-kind principle one more time. Go one more step and hang all blouses and shirts together, all dresses together, and so forth. Go through your categories and organize the individual items by color.

Although closets are the best places for many items, drawers work best for socks, undergarments, scarves, sports apparel, and jewelry. I have had the privilege of cleaning with some of the best-dressed women in the world (their clutter was not anywhere near their closets), and the inside report from these authorities reinforced my own philosophy on drawers. Generally speaking, things like sweaters and T-shirts (which may also be hung) are less likely to get squashed and wrinkled if they are folded and placed on shelves, rather than in drawers.

After you have decluttered and placed clothing in closets, shelves, and drawers, make sure that everything is part of a complete outfit. If things like shoes and belts are missing or if you have tops without bottoms and bottoms without tops, you will know what you are looking for when you go clothes shopping.

SOCKS, PANTYHOSE, AND MORE

It is time to address a clutter-cleaning dilemma that has reached runaway proportions for many people—the sock and pantyhose drawer. The way to happiness just may be through your sock drawer, so forge a path through it and open up more space in your life.

Pantyhose, in particular, are readily available, yet the fear of running out of them has reached near epidemic levels. If you live far from a shopping district or are a hard-to-fit size, then consider buying in bulk by mail and allow yourself to store more than the average amount of pantyhose. But for everyone else, it is unnecessary to have dozens of stockings balled up in drawers upon drawers or bags upon bags. It is generally sufficient to keep two pairs in each color and weight that you normally wear. When your inventory runs low, simply run out and buy more.

After you've worn a pair, wash them out so they are ready for the next wearing. If they tear, toss them. The I'll-wear-them-under-a-pair-of-pants philosophy is not advisable. You'll know the run you are hiding, and clutter cleaning is about being your best.

It is also time to establish a sensible philosophy on socks. Calm yourself of the "just in case" hysteria that you will be without something to cover your feet. If knee-highs are part of your sock wardrobe, treat them as you would pantyhose and have a few untorn pairs in the colors you wear most often. Although it is nice to have ample sports socks (one less excuse to skip exercising), don't overdo it.

For those who are frequently victimized by a sock-gobbling clothes drier, stick to an all-white, all-the-same-style wardrobe of sports socks; they are impossible to mismatch.

Shoes, hats, gloves, jewelry, underwear, and sleepwear all have a tendency to be more cluttered than other forms of clothing and accessories. Now is the time for a one-item-at-a-time review. Once you declutter these types of items, you will be in a good position to assess how they should be organized in an aesthetic way in your environment.

RECYCLING CLOTHES

Now that you have gone through each item, one at a time, and have designated items to be mended, tailored, or cleaned, what are you going to do with all the stuff in the to-be-tossed pile? Your job is not done until you dispense with unwanted clothes—with the appropriate ceremony, of course. Be resourceful about how you will do this and diligent about executing your plan.

Divide all unwanted clothing into categories suitable for family members or friends, donations to a charity, a garage sale, or consignment at a secondhand store. Some clothes will just be trash, in which case just toss them. Do the work necessary to deliver on your promise that the only things that remain in your space are those that you want, need, use, and love. If you have to research the policies of local charity thrift stores and resale or consignment shops to free yourself from unwanted clothes, then just do it. If you have to schedule a date for a garage sale, do the advertising, and execute your plan, then just do it. If you have to make a trip across town to the family member or friend who will receive the clothes or if you need to ship them, then just do it. All these important actions are your entrance ticket to the Ground Zero zone. Being steadfast will pay off in magic and miricles.

If you are the recipient of someone else's clutter cleaning and bags of hand-me-downs show up at your door, keep only what is going to render you compliments. If you can check out hand-me-downs before they come to your house, you will not be stuck with the leftovers. If you are left with them, pass whatever you are not keeping along to someone else or to a charity in the way you have now learned to do—immediately. If the giver does not want these things, you are not obliged to take them either.

FASHION FORWARD: CREATING A WARDROBE THAT WORKS

Once you have rid your closets of clothes that do not fit and are no longer appropriate for the life you are leading, you are at the perfect starting point for building a wardrobe that supports you. First set your sights on organizing your wardrobe in such a way that you are never stuck feeling like you have nothing to wear or don't know where to start. Your goal is to move in and out of your closet effortlessly, saving time and reducing stress. To do so, you have to select clothing that directly relates to how you are fashioning yourself and your life. Developing a clothing philosophy and a shopping strategy will help you accomplish these aims.

How do you develop a clothing philosophy? In my case, *Romper Room,* the television show for kids of yesteryear, provided the foundation for my personal philosophy. When there was precipitation in the air, the actress who played the teacher on the show would dress a Colorforms character in a yellow rain jacket, a matching hat, and red boots. I took it to mean that when it comes to clothes, one should always be prepared.

I also built my clothing philosophy on the direction that I got from another unlikely source—my father. When my mother would bother me about looking unfeminine when I came home to visit from college (wearing a jacket called a "40 below" in reference to the average temperature at Syracuse University), my father would mumble that I should just dress appropriately. I took his advice and kept my coat.

When I made myself a home where the fashion police roam, the latest trends were unavoidable. So I added picking up tips on style from the streets (mostly of New York, but anywhere will do) to my fashion philosophy.

It is quite clear where my advice that you be prepared, dress appropriately, and add a little style in order to be clutter free in the clothing department comes from! You, too, can turn to the past or just look around to define your fashion outlook. Otherwise, the cacophony of voices—your mother, your teachers, your boss, your spouse, fashion magazine editors, MTV, and all the neighbors in your hometown—will join you at your closet door and make a lot of noise, a characteristic of clutter, every time you go to get dressed.

A fashion philosophy will help keep you from being self-conscious about your clothes. Having a shopping strategy will help you select the right ones.

At the beginning of each season, a month or so before you move the clothes in your primary closet to the secondary one (decluttering, cleaning, and pressing them first), assess what you will be doing and how you want to look when the time comes to wear them once again. When you shop, you will be able to focus on filling in any gaps or adding to what you already have.

One of my clients complained that she had a closet full of clothes but still she had nothing to wear. With a little work, we figured out that she tended to shop when her mood was up or down. Thus, her purchases had nothing to do with her actual clothing needs, but were made for emotional reasons. When we cleaned out the clutter and matched her outfits to her goals, we determined that she could live a long, long time without buying another article of clothing. The next time the urge to splurge overtook her, I suggested that she should turn it to her advantage by taking the occasion to stock her kitchen with the dinnerware, glassware, flatware, pots and pans, and other items that she really needed.

That said, when the need for retail therapy strikes, buyer beware. Instead of making random purchases that will fill your closets with future clutter, direct your buying bonanza to what you truly need and use, even if it is not clothing.

When you get into action and go to buy, the less-is-more attitude will go a long way toward keeping you clutter free. Yves St. Laurent may not go down in history as a great philosopher of our times, but he is a fashion guru. I found this St. Laurent quote from a fashion magazine in a cluster of clippings among one client's clutter: "All a woman needs is a black sweater, a black skirt, and a man who loves her on her arm." I told my client that the clipping was worth saving. To me, it says it all.

9

Other Kinds of Clutter

When you know the principles of clutter cleaning and have practiced using them with papers and clothes, you can apply them to other areas of your home and your life.

You may have furniture that is totally wrong for the life you are currently leading, but to which you have become so accustomed that it has never occurred to you to get rid of it. Or perhaps there is a VCR you still cannot program, an old record turntable sitting around, or other appliances and equipment that you cannot or do not use. Another problem you may encounter is that while you are becoming clutter free, others in your household are not yet enlightened. Or perhaps you have piles of photographs or boxes full of books, memorabilia, or valuables that you don't know what to do with.

Although I share my point of view about this other clutter, I urge you to adapt the clutter-cleaning principles to fit your own circumstances and personal style. As you travel through to the land of the clutter free, establish your own initiatives about everything. You will know you are doing things right when you approach your clutter as you might a challenging jigsaw puzzle—with a sense of wonder of how it will ever get done, a clear picture of the end result, and a spirit of adventure.

JUNKY, BULKY, UGLY FURNITURE

One of the interesting things about cleaning clutter is that the more you clean, the more you uncover. Sometimes what surfaces is the most obvious. With paper out of the way and clothes that actually fit in your closet, for example, you may find junky, bulky, ugly furniture staring you in the face.

This furniture may have followed you from a college dorm as a hand-me-down from your mother, a sibling, or an aunt. Or perhaps most of your stuff came from flea markets or thrift stores. For instance in New York, it is not uncommon to pick up furniture that has been tossed out on the street or abandoned in basements of buildings. Whatever your furniture's history, when you look at it with a fresh eye after clutter cleaning, you may find it glaringly wrong for the future you envision.

Take a close look around. Are pieces missing handles, have you hung on to chairs with broken legs, or do you have an ugly table stuck in a corner where it is collecting clutter? If the truth be told, you have long ago dismissed all these items, yet they remain in your space. Whatever regret or sorrow it may bring, get ready to bid them good-bye.

Begin to route all items of this nature to an area you designate as the morgue. After having hunted down this type of clutter through your entire house or apartment, it is time to dispose of it all. Brace yourself, breathe, hold a funeral or do a ceremony, but don't hold on. Call the Salvation Army. Empty space is ahead, and it can bring you more joy than your junk.

APPLIANCES AND EQUIPMENT: UNUSED, UNWANTED, AND NOT WORKING

Appliances and equipment that don't work, aren't used, and are obsolete can begin to loom as large as junky, bulky, ugly furniture. When smaller types of clutter disappear and your environment comes more into focus, you may find a VCR you don't know how to operate, a vacuum cleaner that doesn't work, and a turntable that is a dinosaur.

I think of appliances and electronic equipment as generating negative energy if they are not working for you. Such negative energy is taxing to your senses and dulls your consciousness. Clutter cleaning is about raising consciousness.

Start by fixing broken equipment. If you don't want to fix it, toss it or give it away. If you are hanging on to equipment you've never learned to use (like the VCR), read the instructions, even if you have to call the manufacturer to get a booklet, and then put the instructions in a file. Do not keep the instruction booklet alongside or underneath the appliance. What about objects that are too good to toss but that you just don't want? Give them away to friends or a charity or sell them.

I once had a VCR that I took to a repair shop for an estimate. The repairman said it would cost $75 to fix, so I took it back home again, thinking the price was too high. I waited another couple of months. I couldn't do anything with the machine, but I felt bad throwing it out. So I took it to the store again, and the repair had now doubled in cost. I immediately found someone who fixed it for less. The moral of the story is get equipment and appliances out of your way or working; there could be a cost involved in waiting!

OTHER PEOPLE'S STUFF

You're well on your way to freeing yourself from clutter, but now you want your dad to clean up his act, your mom to end her pack-rat ways, your husband to straighten up, your wife to stop amassing a mess, and your roommate to cease cramping your style, so you can be relieved of *their* stuff. Well, I hate to tell you, but there is little you can do about other people's clutter. The best you can hope for is that as you get on a clutter-free path, your change is likely to have a positive effect on the people around you. Once you surround yourself with things that reflect and uplift the real and enlightened you, you will have a stronger base of operation from which to extend yourself to those around you. You can even broaden your horizons and start cleaning up clutter, wherever and whatever it may be. You can rally the family to clean their living spaces or be a cheerleader for a clutter-free workplace.

If the results of your clutter cleaning are insufficient to motivate your spouse, roommate, or kids, then start by taking some time to itemize exactly what it is that's bothering you in specific terms—the top of the dresser is unruly, the garage is overloaded, or the papers in the den make it uncomfortable. Then call a meeting to share your vision for the way you want to live, ask your partner what his or her vision is, and use your list of specifics to identify what is not working for you. Then see if by calmly discussing the issue of clutter you can set mutual goals and negotiate actions that you both can take to correct the situation and fulfill shared objectives. If the other party (or parties) is not open to talking and working in this fashion, do not concentrate on cleaning clutter with them. Instead, just open up the lines of communication to make room to clean clutter.

As action is the only thing that will remove your physical clutter, talking is the way of opening space in your relationships so that everyone thrives. As you come into yourself after decluttering, some relationships may need to be reassessed. The object of cleaning clutter is not to throw things away or to get rid of relationships. But as you reshape your environment so it enhances, rather than thwarts, your goals, some relationships may require redirection. Regardless of whether your relationships were good or bad before you cleaned clutter, some things may have to change afterward. For example, if you were the one who always did the grocery shopping and the errands in your family, but your schedule is now too full with courses or career-counseling sessions to make room for what you want, you're going to have to ask for help.

KID'S STUFF

I know I wrote earlier in this book that my philosophy of clutter cleaning is not about "a place for everything and everything in its place." But the one area where I do think that approach is useful is in children's rooms.

Most kids' rooms have great potential to look like war zones. It is extremely useful to have a trunk or closets in which to store toys, books, and games. When it is time to play, all the apparatus is easily pulled out, but when a play period has ended and it's time to eat dinner, get ready for homework, or prepare for bed, all that kid stuff can be easily stashed.

Kids' toys and clothes quickly become clutter if you don't stay on top of the accumulation. Apply your clutter-cleaning skills to your child's abandoned toys or outgrown clothes. If your child is old enough to help, consider this training a terrific legacy.

No sooner do you buy clothes than they grow small. Be sensible with your purchases, allowing some flexibility for the pressure of trends. But as is always the case in cleaning clutter there are times you have to put your foot down and say no. If you are expecting another child to grow into clothes you have that they're not ready for, store them appropriately in an attic or in a chest so they are out of the way until they are ready to be worn.

Kids have paper, too. You can plant the seeds that will help them develop good decluttering skills if you set aside one bin for each child in which to keep their papers. You will begin to teach your children not only organizational skills, but respect for their space and that of others. Teach them the filing methods you learn as a going-away present before they enter college.

PHOTOGRAPHS

Stray photographs are a common form of clutter. In fact, most people have oodles of them in boxes and bags stuffed into drawers. Most of us want to keep photographs to hand down the family legacy, to make sense of our lives, and to remember good times and good people.

Saving photographs is a way really to honor and even create your past. You can tell the story of your life through your photographs, and it is fun to have them at your fingertips so you can appreciate them and share them with other people. If they're stashed in boxes or bags stuffed somewhere, you won't be able to find them or enjoy them.

Pick a way to store your photographs that will allow you to look at them whenever you want. Arrange them in an appealing way—in sequences by place, person, year, or occasion or in a collage.

Albums and photo file boxes are the two most common ways to store photographs. New technology provides another fancy option—photographs can be put on compact disks, and then you can view them on your computer and E-mail them to your relatives or friends. You can manipulate the images, too, deleting someone you don't like from a scene or changing the color of the dress or tie. You really can have fun.

Some people consider it bad luck to throw away any photographs. I don't. If you took a beautiful shot of your foot, a photograph is blurred or came with a Christmas card and you don't *really* want to save it, or you have enough of one series of shots, feel free just to toss them. If you wish, send the ones you no longer want to someone who would appreciate them or to the trash with a special blessing.

Photographs are reflections of the past, and decluttering them can put the past where it belongs—behind you. Once I bought five like-kind albums that fit uniformly on a bookshelf so I could get all the photographs I had in boxes and bags mounted in a convenient place. In the process, I was shocked to discover that for an entire decade I had not taken any photographs. I discovered that I'd stopped taking photographs when the camera, which a former boyfriend had given me, broke. Since being thorough in my clutter-cleaning effort entailed fixing the camera, I finally took it in for repair. I was surprised to learn that it just needed new batteries. It was the relationship, not the camera, that had been broken. I am happily taking photographs again.

Photographs are probably last on people's lists when it comes to cleaning clutter because they seem the least pressing. But this book is about going 100 percent. A rainy afternoon or a snowy Sunday is an ideal time to weather this type of clutter. Relax and enjoy yourself and take a few moments to reflect. Trust that there will be a miracle and look forward to seeing what it is.

BOOKS

It is difficult to think of books as clutter. But the truth is, they can overwhelm your space. Clients ask three main questions about books: Can I throw books away? How do I select which ones to keep? and How do I incorporate them into my home?

On the one hand, there is no reason not to keep all your books as long as they add to your life. But books don't *have* to be forever. If you have too many or you have some that are no longer meaningful, weed them out. As with your other clutter, go through your books one at a time and determine which have relevance to you now. Donate or sell those that have none. Shelve the others in whatever way works for you.

I used to refrain from buying books because I had no place to put them. When I redecorated my apartment, I bought handsome wall cabinets with plenty of shelves for books. My books aren't especially decorative, so I added frosted-glass doors to the shelves.

I know people who take pride in their books. Their books add beauty and soul to a room, and they are conversation pieces. If this sounds like you, make them a central part of your design scheme.

The same considerations apply to storing videotapes, audio-tapes, and compact disks. Make your selections one at a time, map out a storage strategy, and be creative about eliminating what you no longer need or want.

MEMORABILIA

Many of us hold on to things with sentimental value—things that belonged to someone important in our lives, things that remind us of special events and places. Memorabilia are in the eye of the beholder and can be almost anything, from ticket stubs and photographs to autographs and bronzed baby shoes. The way to keep memorabilia from turning into clutter is to designate them as such and separate them from items you use in your daily life.

If your memorabilia are important to you, find a creative way to store them that will honor them, yet not create a road-block of any kind. You may even start a family tradition. One client started a treasure chest for her children because she was sentimental about clothes that they wore at certain milestones in their lives. The treasure chest is a new family tradition.

Maybe your memorabilia is a collection of little "things." Think about buying an attractive box in which to keep them.

Scrapbooks are a good choice for ticket stubs and other flat items. They are great for teenagers, who can really get creative while saving prom programs, letters, drawings, and more. You may be able to train your kids early to save their artwork, papers, and other stuff in their scrapbooks, rather than all over their rooms.

Memorabilia have their place. Just contain them in an inventive way that reflects their meaning to you.

VALUABLES

After years of collecting, fashion designer Norma Kamali wanted to create more room for a fresh perspective on her life and her work. Her charge was not an easy one because her passion for collecting ran deep—Art Deco perfume bottles, antique clothing (including 750 hats), original designs from her home furnishings collection, Empire and Biedermeier antiques, rococo tables, a Louis XV-style ormolu chandelier, and the set of encyclopedias her mother bought with coupons from the A & P. Her collections filled a triplex apartment in New York and several warehouses.

"There are things I want to do to change the way I look at clothing, at design. And to do that, I have to change the way I live and change my environment. . . . Something is about to happen in my life and what I do. I don't know what it is, but I know what I have to do before it happens. And every time something goes, I'm opening myself up for whatever it is that is new," said the designer in a February 1996 article in the *New York Observer*. Kamali's solution was to hold a sale at Christie's, the famous auction house.

Whether or not you have Christie's-quality furnishings like Kamali, you can take your inspiration from her. Trade in what you once treasured for what is next on the horizon. I don't recommend taking expensive items down to the local thrift store in exchange for a receipt for a tax deduction—this is not the most prudent way to handle pricey stuff. Disposing of valuables requires a bit more effort than getting rid of less costly items. Take a leap of faith, do some creative thinking, and get busy surveying your options.

Have a creative session with yourself and ask other people for ideas. Should you approach an auction house, advertise in a specialty magazine, sell outright to a collector, or place an item in a consignment shop? Use your ingenuity and apply your research and study skills to the problem. If you have no experience, this will be an educational opportunity. Then simply commit yourself to a course of action. If you're having trouble committing, assess whether what you are making room for in your life is more important than holding on. Try to keep your attention on the real payoff and continue to press yourself to move ahead.

A student in one of my classes wanted to get rid of a collection of crystal she and her husband had accumulated over the years. As we talked about what she should do, she revealed that she was a member of a collector's organization that published a magazine. When I pointed out that she could always advertise in the magazine, it became clear that her problem wasn't really in finding a solution but in letting go.

Sometimes solutions present themselves once you've made up your mind what you are going to do. For example, a friend inherited a record collection from a long-time family friend who had just died. She decided to sell the collection, not for the money, but to pass the records along to someone who would value them. Once she made the decision to sell them, she noticed an advertisement in a neighborhood newspaper placed by a record collector that otherwise would not have caught her eye. She sold part of her collection to him, and he was able to refer her to someone else who was interested in all the others.

10

Decluttering Room by Room

The decluttering principles that you've learned in the earlier chapters can be applied to every room and every item in your house or apartment. But certain rooms tend to require more clutter-cleaning attention than others.

Bedrooms, bathrooms, kitchens, attics, and basements are all item-intensive places—and thus are also clutter hot spots.

In attics and basements, in particular, it is easy to slip into the "out of sight, out of mind" attitude. But a little conscientiousness will help keep these repositories of junk from becoming traps for old energy. Likewise, garages and sheds can readily become dumping grounds for everything that you relegate to the "miscellaneous" category—a red flag for clutter. But even these areas can be a showcase for how well you bring your mastery of clutter cleaning to all areas of your home and your life.

THE MASTER BEDROOM

These days, people use the master bedroom for virtually everything: from a sleep sanctuary to a dining table to a home office to a laundry-sorting and ironing center. I prefer to preserve the bedroom solely as a place of serenity and intimacy. It is from this perspective that I suggest that few things other than essential furnishings and select accents remain in a bedroom after you clean clutter. Everything in the bedroom should foster soothing comfort for rest, relaxation, or romance.

Books, magazines, a television, paperwork, or miscellaneous paraphernalia, for example, even if orderly and not strewn around the room, need not be in permanent residence in the bedroom. My feeling is that these items should be there on a temporary, by-invitation-only basis. Otherwise, they can be distracting aesthetically and energetically.

It may seem that what I am suggesting is drastic, but the sacred space you create for yourself and whomever else will be worth it. If you have decluttered your closets and papers and have had some practice putting the clutter-cleaning principles to work in other areas of your home, decluttering the master bedroom will not be as difficult as it seems.

Start by putting all your clothes and shoes away. Then move systematically across the surfaces of bedside tables and bureaus, setting items on a new path. For example, if the bedside table is the place you empty the pockets of your pants or the contents of your purse, it is simple enough to direct receipts to your home office area and ultimately, to a file. Find an attractive container for loose change, which you can store in a cabinet or inside a drawer; when it is filled to capacity, roll the money in wrappers and buy yourself a treat. A handsome jewelry case or jar for frequently worn accessories can be attractive on a dresser top, but if you have a lot of jewelry, consider devoting a drawer to it or invest in a compartmentalized jewelry system that hangs in a closet (you can find them in catalogs). Books or magazines that find their way to the bedroom for a one-night stand can be housed in an accent piece, but use it for the ones you are presently reading. As you clear space, you may want to introduce calming or pleasure-enhancing elements, such as flowers, candles, or pot-pourri.

My work with one client, Maxine, started in her bedroom because she was making room in her life for more intimacy with her boyfriend. It was interesting that her bedroom contained the largest mass of her clutter. She had a mound of boxes about five feet high in the center of her bedroom that were ever-so-carefully covered with a pink sheet in an attempt to make it seem as if they were not really there. At the end of a long day of burrowing through her stuff like two groundhogs, we stood in the doorway of her bedroom and admired it because it looked as fresh as a hotel room at check-in time, except for one large picture turned backward and leaning against the wall.

I walked over to the picture and turned it around to see what it was. Under the beautiful image of a woman in a fetal position were these words: *A Woman Giving Birth to Herself.* The space that Maxine had created in her bedroom allowed her true self to emerge, forming the basis of a new chapter in her relationship with a man whom she wanted to embrace more dearly.

BATHROOMS TO PAMPER YOURSELF IN

The bathroom is susceptible to clutter because it is here that so many bottles, jars, boxes, tubes, and containers of everything from shampoos and conditioners, paper goods, soaps, perfumes, medications, remedies, and emergency treatments to sewing, jewelry, and linens reside. Though many items are appropriately stashed here, these generally small rooms are usually asked to store far more than their space would dictate.

Because bathrooms are usually common rooms that are used daily by more than one member of a household, don't complicate your life by leaving a decluttering project halfway finished here. In most cases, bathroom clutter can be dealt with in a single two- to four-hour clutter-cleaning session.

Decluttering the bathroom starts by isolating specific areas first (under the sink and the medicine cabinet where the clutter accumulates) and then applying the like-kind-things-together principle to each. For example, first pull everything out from under the sink. Cluster the under-the-sink items into like-kind groupings, spreading the groupings out on the floor in a hallway or other room so you have space to work. Sort items by category (shampoos with shampoos, medications with medications); then conduct an item-by-item review, designating stuff to be discarded, given away, or kept.

Next open the medicine chest. Add items you are keeping from the medicine chest to the like-kind groupings, going through the same process as for the under-the-sink items. In addition to making like-kind groupings, check the expiration dates on all items (not just medications) and get rid of the old ones.

Repeat this process until all areas of the bathroom have been emptied and the items have been reviewed, grouped, and dealt with. By working this way, things may seem to get messier before they get cleaner, but that is a normal part of the process. Before you put the items you are keeping away, reassess your storage needs and ask yourself if your present storage arrangements really suit your needs. I recommend storing some small like-kind items together in clear plastic storage containers that can be easily labeled and stacked under the sink or cabinet.

Once you have thoroughly decluttered the bathroom, it should be fairly simple to maintain it if you also reassess your buying habits. Many of us are compulsive when it comes to purchasing items, such as makeup, cosmetics, and sundries—the advertisements are seductive and prey on our insecurities. When purchased one item at a time, these items seem harmless. But it is easy to amass huge collections of redundant items that fill your bathroom and add up substantially in cost.

I had a client who insisted that her beauty products and cosmetics (which filled laundry baskets that lined three walls of her bedroom) were her passion. In this case, overconsumption was so out of hand that it was imperiling her marriage. This wasn't a passion; it was a problem. What was she going to do, convert her bedroom into a cosmetics and beauty supply warehouse? A more realistic approach is to exercise restraint, declutter what you have, and formulate new makeup-buying tactics. Keep decluttering your makeup supply until everything you have is something that you regularly use. When you get to this point, it is unlikely that you will need more than one cosmetic bag.

It is easy to be seduced into thinking that muds, masks, cleansers, moisturizers, foundations, powders, eyeliners, and gloss, each with its own corresponding brush and pad, are your keys to lasting youth, beauty, and happiness. But decluttering is a time to develop a more secure sense of yourself. Self-assurance is more appealing than all the makeup you can buy.

Another pointer that can help reduce bathroom clutter is to have a compact, packed travel kit stored under the sink or in a bathroom cabinet ready to go when you are. Stock the kit with one each of a travel-size shampoo, conditioner, liquid soap, tube of toothpaste, and blow dryer, as well as a toothbrush, shaving cream and razors, tanning lotion, contact lens solution, styling gel, cleansing pads, a small sewing kit, and so forth. Having a packed travel kit on hand means that you will have one less thing to remember in the scurry to leave home and will be less likely to be caught in the dead of night in a far-off city without having all your bases covered.

THE KITCHEN: THE HEALTHY HEART OF YOUR HOME

Kitchens are places where clutter seems to grow to fill the space, and then some. But as in other rooms, your decluttering procedure will have a predictable path. As you did in the bathroom, try to get to Ground Zero in a single two- to four-hour session. If you have more to tackle in the kitchen than one session will allow, isolate areas of the kitchen and tackle one area at a time, and use the one-item-at-a-time approach.

Areas to isolate include the refrigerator, the pantry, the utensil drawer, shelves for dishes and food, and your junk drawer—every kitchen has one. Spreading things out on countertops, tabletops, or even the floor helps you in the sorting and evaluating process.

Don't forget to declutter the area under the sink, and like any other part of the item-intensive kitchen, be bold when you approach it. Take a deep breath and dive in, putting like-kind things together, assessing what you need and what you want from what is trash. Use decluttering as an occasion to take inventory of your cleaning supplies. You may find that you have a surplus of bags of all shapes and sizes jammed into this area. This is a good time to develop a "bag policy."

By a bag policy, I mean whittle down your supply of bags to the bare essentials. Do you really reuse shopping or grocery bags, or do your good intentions keep you oversupplied? Since I generally cart things to and fro in a sturdy canvas bag, I decline a bag from a store when I can toss a purchase into my tote. I do keep a few bags on hand in several different sizes, just in case. You may have to reconcile your environmental conscience and your bag policy, but if you do not find a way to limit your intake of bags and toss those you do not need, they'll overwhelm you.

Now turn to your junk drawer and consider the possibility of turning it into a satellite office of sorts—a communications center. First, go through the drawer using your decluttering technique. Then, install a desk tray for pens and pencils, paper clips, a notepad and Post-Its, a telephone book or electronic organizer with frequently dialed telephone numbers, a few rubber bands, a pair of scissors, and a roll of tape. You may want to keep a binder clip there to hold important receipts, such as those for repairs or the dry cleaner. Send your take-out menus to a file in your home office area, a better place for papers than the kitchen. Things, such as batteries, extension cords, nails, and screws, which are commonly tossed into a junk drawer, can be put on the path to the tool kit or kept in a separate drawer of like-kind things. If you are unwilling to let go of a haven for so-called junk, designate no more than one drawer for this purpose.

When you clean your pantry, group foods in like-kind categories so it is easy to see what you have in stock. Put pastas with pastas, soups with soups, cereals with cereals, and so on. It is easy to overstock—two years' worth of mayonnaise but no salt—when you have no idea what you have on hand because of the mess in your cabinets. If you can easily see what kitchen staples you are short on and think about what you will be serving your family in advance of your shopping trip, then you will buy what you will actually eat, making your meals fresher and ultimately healthier. Rethink your buying habits wherever you have too much excess—whether in the bathroom, the kitchen, or your clothing closets—because this is one source of clutter that can be fairly easy to correct once you are aware that it exists.

ATTICS AND BASEMENTS

In the clothing business, the quality of a garment is measured by how finely tailored it is on the inside, the part that only the wearer sees. The same principle applies to decluttering areas of your home you don't frequent, such as your attic or basement. I call these areas the underbelly of the home. Give them as much attention as the rooms you really live in.

People have a tendency to treat attics and basements as

receptacles for trash, haphazardly or blindly tossing things into them. If you are fortunate enough to have these areas, don't abuse them, use them. Attics and basements are great places to store memorabilia, treasure chests, camping and ski equipment, and off-season clothing if you don't have secondary closet space. Christmas, Halloween, or New Year's hats, horns, decorations, ornaments, wrappings, and unused greeting cards can hibernate happily in these areas, too.

Think of your attic or basement as analogous to the storage and resource files you learned to create in chapter 6, Processing Papers. Just because they hold things you don't need to use daily, they should still be thoughtfully set up so they function well for you as soon as you are ready. Neatly place items to be stored in the attic or basement in like-kind groupings and store them in boxes or plastic bins (not in bags) that can be stacked and moved easily. Label what you can for easy identification. Set up clothing racks for hanging off-season or fat and skinny clothes, putting them first in garment bags to protect them from dust and dirt.

Cleaning below the surface in out-of-the-way areas is an essential part of the decluttering process. When someone asks me why I am cleaning a drawer instead of a tabletop or a secondary closet instead of the primary one first, I say I'm doing root canal. Cleaning the back-end areas first often gives you the room to spread out more of what you decide to keep when you declutter other spots. If a closet is filled to its limit, take a step back and clean the attic first as part of the process. After the attic is decluttered, you'll have more room for overflow items from your primary closet.

Once the chaos in attics and basements is eliminated, you will get the added benefit of more soothing energy emanating from above and below. Diligence in clutter cleaning these areas demonstrates that you are willing to go the greatest length to lighten up. Since actions speak louder than words, someone up there is bound to get your message.

GARAGES AND SHEDS

Garages and sheds usually hold particular kinds of things—car wax, oil, and other automotive supplies, lawn and garden equipment, tools, and bicycles. To declutter these areas, use the like-kind-things-together approach. Put screwdrivers all together, nails with nails, screws with screws, and bolts with bolts, paintbrushes and rollers in one place, and car stuff on the same shelf. You will probably find that once you are done, you can even park your car in the garage, which is usually an impossible feat for the overcluttered.

Approach a shed in the same way as you do the garage. Put all the trowels and other hand tools together, clean and stack the flowerpots, have a place for gardening gloves, keep spare lawnmower blades together, and put shovels with shovels and hoes with hoes.

Keeping fertilizers and pesticides all in one place makes it easier to handle and store them safely and correctly—you will never lose track of half-used bottles of toxic materials. Having your shed organized will ensure that your hobby remains a pleasure and doesn't become a headache.

Although garages and sheds are part of your private property, they are the most vulnerable to the scrutiny of others. Why not take the opportunity to enhance your standing in the community and impress your neighbors? How many times have you driven down a block and found yourself oohing and ahhing over a well-appointed garage with its door proudly flung open? Don't have a moment of doubt that such a garage can belong to you.

HOBBY AREAS

Sewing rooms, workshops, painting studios, and other areas designated for working on hobbies are not off limits for a dedicated declutterer. Your clutter-cleaning intentions may be easily dismissed during your mad flurries of artistic inspiration, but clutter is still clutter, and we are on a mission to clean it up.

Many people, especially those who are particularly creative, resist structure, thinking it will inhibit them. One of the ironies of cleaning clutter is that exactly the opposite is true. Building structure sets you free. When you have a place for your brushes, hooks for your tools, and baskets and bins to hold your supplies, these items are handy yet out of the way, so the environment can become to you what a blank canvas is to an artist—a clear space for a fresh start.

Designate areas to work on your hobbies; declutter your supplies; organize everything that you use; and when the time comes, indulge yourself to your heart's content. Then, like a child after play, put your supplies away so when you return, you aren't faced with the remains of your last project—you can plunge right in.

Decluttering these spaces can be painful because many hobbies involve lots of small pieces and details. Such is the case with sewing rooms, which contain tiny buttons, pins, intricate little fasteners, and trims. Although it may be unnerving to declutter them, it's worth the effort. Just put the like-kind-things principle into practice and forge ahead with the vision of what you are making room for in your life. Press yourself to be thorough and leave no stone unturned.

11

Prepare for the Unexpected

Once you work your clutter-cleaning magic throughout your house, take precautions to manage the clutter so it does not reach epidemic proportions again. But sometimes clutter is uncontrollable and unforeseen. A natural disaster like a flood or a self-imposed catastrophe, such as having the house painted, can lead to a crescendo of clutter. But what appears to be a clutter-cleaning setback can be viewed as an opportunity to weed through your things.

Clutter cleaning is not always something you do because you have no other recourse. You can use it deliberately to ease a transition. For instance, anytime you are on the threshold of change—moving to a new apartment, merging households with a new mate, dividing up belongings when you divorce or break up, adding a little one to the family, or entering your retirement years—clutter cleaning can help with life's changes. It gives us an opportunity to clean and, when necessary, an opportunity to heal.

MOVING, REFURBISHING, RECOVERING FROM A DISASTER

Moving offers the perfect opportunity to declutter, and you can do it as you pack. As you pack the kitchen, for example, think about whether you really want to move the bent old spatula, the grimy cookie sheet, or the cracked serving platter. This may be your chance to send those things to the thrift store or, if they're in really bad shape, the trash. As you pack each item, ask yourself whether you really want it in your new living space.

This principle applies to everything and every room you pack. Declutter and file your papers as you pack them in portable file boxes, so you will be ready to set up a new office immediately in your new place. Start this process as far in advance of your move as is reasonable, so you will not be rushed. The stress of adapting to a change of location need not be compounded by decluttering.

Pack everything in boxes. They are sturdy, space efficient, stackable, and easier to move than shopping bags. Even throw last-minute items into a box and label it "clutter" as a reminder that it is an assortment of jumbled, unlike things.

I had one client who decluttered before moving to a new apartment. She packed carefully, and when the movers came, they were able to load her belongings and deliver them to her new apartment within two hours. Good packing makes the transition swift and painless.

Paint jobs are another opportunity for lightening up. Although you aren't changing locations, paint jobs can transform your space. But be sure to pack for a paint job as you would for a move—declutter as you pack things in boxes. One friend ended up sleeping in her living room for two years after she had her place painted because she hadn't unpacked and put her rooms back together. When she finally got down to cleaning her clutter, the first step was to clear a path to her bedroom!

MAJOR MILESTONES IN LIFE

When you get married, when a new baby comes, when children get their own rooms, when older children leave the nest, and when you retire—all are opportunities for clutter cleaning. Either you will be moving or your household will be changing significantly. Clutter cleaning can help you handle growing or changing responsibilities. It is a way to reorient yourself.

Marriage, for instance, means merging his and her closets. If two people can successfully do so, their relationship shows great promise. When a new baby comes, it's a nesting time, a time to prepare for inevitable, irreversible change. And when toddlers suddenly become preteens it is yet another time to shift your living space.

I had clients who lived in a five-story townhouse. When the children were babies, the whole family lived on the second floor, so the children could be next door to their parents. When the children were old enough, they got their own rooms, and the parents got more privacy when they expanded the use of all their space. The children were involved in the clutter-cleaning game plan. They began by answering the question: What are you making room for in your life by clutter cleaning? The younger child wanted a bigger play area, and the older child wanted to read more chapter books. The mother was going back to work, and the father just wanted everyone to be happy. The family was growing and changing, and they altered their living arrangements to accommodate that fact. They rearranged the house for the family to grow.

Parents and their teenage children also may find that creating room in the home to spread out a little makes everyone happier. When one client's teenage daughter wanted more space and her own telephone, the parents moved her upstairs to the third floor, which had been used as an attic. Before they did so, they had to clear out the basement to make room for things that had been in the attic and widen a doorway to make the upper level a luxury bedroom and homework suite. Then the younger brother moved into his sister's bedroom, and his old room was turned into a family office/homework station.

When your children leave the nest altogether, life—and living space—changes again, and you should change with it. I've met retired couples who still have bedrooms with pink sheets and ruffles or baseball bats and pennants even though their children are married and have children of their own. Change keeps you vital. Instead of thinking it's all over when your kids leave the house, look at it as a time to reinvent.

I had one pair of clients in this situation. Over time, they turned one child's bedroom into a home office, which enabled the wife, a business owner, to start a satellite office of her company at home. A granddaughter desk, a miniature of her own in primary colors decorated with dolls instead of business accouterments, made space for work and play when little visitors arrived. Overnight guests find that the office couch is a convertible bed. The other child's room was turned into a combination office, gym, and television lounging area for her recently retired husband. The couple still has a third bedroom for other guests and a blow-up mattress in the closet in case of a crowd.

Another client was a city government employee and had been strategizing about her retirement for years. When the time came to retire, she stayed in bed and watched daytime talk shows for months instead of picking up and moving to a new city as she had always wanted. When we toured the clutter in her apartment, I kept pointing to things and inquiring, "What is this?" "It is for the garage sale I'm going to have," she'd answer. After I asked the same question nine or ten times and received the identical answer, it occurred to me to ask, "How long have you been planning this garage sale?" "I had one ten years ago with a friend of mine, and since then we have thought we would do it again," she replied.

I suggested that she call her friend, pick a date, and execute her plan. She did so immediately. Her aim was to relocate, and cleaning her clutter lightened her burden, which facilitated her move.

Cleaning clutter is an excellent way to forge change and usher in a new life. Use clutter cleaning as a tool to ground you when the winds of change blow. In so doing, you will be more likely to greet the unknown with open arms, ready to experience the glory of living in the moment.

BELONGINGS OF THE DECEASED

This is a tough one. Going through the belongings of a departed loved one means dealing with the loss all over again. It may take you more than thirty seconds to decide what you're going to do with any one item, but a scrupulous plan and attention to the project can be healing.

Generally speaking, I recommend that you address the belongings of a deceased person soon after his or her death. It can help you to accept that the person is gone. If you are able to relate to your loved one on a spiritual, rather than a material, plane, you may have an easier time dealing with the possessions.

One client called me three years after her husband died to help her remove his clothing from a main closet in their bedroom. She insisted that we take the long way around, cleaning all her closets first. The day we finally began working on his stuff, mayhem broke out: Her dog was hit by a car and killed when the housekeeper took him out for a walk. Needless to say, the dog's death distracted her from the process, and I don't know if she ever got back on track. During this period, I kept seeing what appeared to be a ghost of her husband in the park and on the street. I may have been imagining things, but it was one of those situations that cause you to wonder. What is clear, however, is that her procrastination in dealing with her husband's clothing is evidence that she had difficulty facing her loss.

On another occasion, I was working with a client who had extensive clutter under a built-in loft bed. Despite major clutter in this space, I was drawn to a small sewing box amidst the mess. As I soon learned, this box was a tailoring kit that had belonged to her deceased ex-father-in-law. It was a historic item, which seemed to emit a lot of old and unhappy energy into her space. She had long forgotten that she owned this item, and she had no sentimental attachment to it. She decided to restore the vitality of her space by letting the kit go.

Perhaps you have a family heirloom that doesn't fit into your current environment but you want to save it for your children. Try to store the item in the basement, attic, or elsewhere, where it won't take up room in your living space (an outside storage facility may be worthwhile). Although it can be difficult to do, let an item go if it has no place in your life.

I had one client who kept a sewing machine in the middle of the living room of her tiny apartment. You had to edge around it to cross from one side of the room to the other. The woman did not sew, and the machine was broken, but it was the only thing she had that belonged to her mother, who had died twenty years before. In the way it was being treated, the machine was more of an intrusion than an honored memory. I suggested that my client, a photographer, take a picture of the sewing machine and contribute the actual item to a trade school, where it could have a new, useful life.

Another client was emotionally crippled by the stuff her father left behind. Although she lived elsewhere much of the time, she had an entire apartment filled with his things ten years after he had died. He had a valuable art collection, rare books, and some auction-quality ceramics and artifacts, all mixed in with flea-market stuff. The daughter didn't know what was valuable and what was not and just could not deal with disposing of any of it. She was so preoccupied with her dead father's belongings that she couldn't focus on her own life.

Although dispersing the belongings of those who have died can be unbearably sad, it can open the space to begin a new and bright chapter of your life.

Learning Skills At a Glance

Here are my nine basic clutter-cleaning principles. Use them and create your own signature clutter-cleaning style.

1. *Handle One Item at a Time*
2. *A path for everything, everything on a path.* Instead of being concerned about finding a proper place for things, get them moving in the right direction to move your clutter-cleaning process along.
3. *Don't cover your tracks.* Once you clutter clean an area, don't reintroduce clutter there.
4. *Like-kind things, like-kind energies together.* Put paper with paper, clothes with clothes, loose change with loose change, and so on. The energy of physical objects that have no relevance to your life closes down space; objects with an energy that coincides with your own have a generative quality.

5. *Take breaks.* If you get tired or bored while cleaning, take a five- to ten-minute break to restore your energy.

6. *Leave no stone unturned.* Be thorough in cleaning one isolated area at a time. Go 100 percent.

7. *Dispose of things with some ceremony.* When you toss garbage or give away what you don't want, it is cause to celebrate. Dispose of stuff with panache.

8. *Empty space always gets filled.* Don't be afraid of the empty space you create by cleaning. It will get filled with what is good for you.

9. *Acknowledge the steps you have taken.* Pat yourself on the back when you make progress. You deserve it.

A few specifics to refresh you:

- To declutter papers, set up a system for filing that reflects your projects, goals, and interests. Three main hubs for storing paper in a clutter-free environment are the file cabinet; the system for recording names, numbers, and addresses; and the in-box. When the three-part paper-processing exercise (sorting, prefiling, and final filing) is complete, you will be left with a manageable volume of papers and a workable filing system.

- You know you've succeeded in decluttering your clothes when your wardrobe reflects what you do and defines and expresses who you are. Start by removing all empty hangers from closets and reassess clothing one item at a time by putting it to this test:

  - Is it appropriate for an activity you engage in or want to?
  - Does it fit?
  - Is it in season?
  - Is it cleaned, mended, and pressed?
  - Is it in fashion, or does it fit your lifestyle?
  - Will you wear it?

- When you declutter bathrooms and kitchens, try to complete the job in a single session and work on one area at a time. Attics, basements, garages or sheds, and hobby areas offer the opportunity to be 100 percent clutter free.

- Furniture, appliances, and equipment, kids' stuff, photographs, books, memorabilia, and valuables can be clutter if you don't address them.

- Moving, refurbishing, recovering from a natural disaster, or dealing with the belongings of the deceased are times to declutter open space for a new future.

Part III

LIVING CLUTTER FREE

12

Routine Practices and Disciplines

If you have traveled the distance in cleaning your clutter, you are not the same person who started out on this journey. You've ascended mountains of resistance and papers. You've swum in vast oceans of tears of joy and sadness and clothes. You've fought off your evil demons and unwanted birthday gifts. You've gone on your hands and knees to the far reaches of your sock drawer, your attic, and your soul. You've blasted through barriers and the basement. You've been on a quest for freedom, and you've triumphed!

The first step to staying free from clutter is to realize you are not living in the same skin as you were when you started cleaning clutter. Treat yourself with newfound respect—you can trust yourself to get to Ground Zero! It may feel strange at first, but you have created a sacred space and discovered that the light at the end of the tunnel is your own.

Although you may have traveled one step at a time through

your clutter, you may start to find yourself moving at an even faster speed—one leap at a time. The principle is the same, and so is the need to stay grounded and keep decluttering. Now, however, anytime you are about to take a leap forward, you can seek clutter before it seeks you. Look for opportunities to uncover what underlies any mess. In the process you can continue to learn new things about yourself and expand the space in which to grow. As you step into new territory, your exposure to the ecstasy that exists there will be enhanced without clutter being in the way.

There are routine clutter-cleaning disciplines and practices—from handling the daily mail and dealing with magazines, catalogs, spring cleaning, unpacking from trips, and doing laundry—that will usher you along your path of clutter-free living. These cleaning skills are fundamental, but they are just the beginning.

DAILY MAIL, E-MAIL, AND PHONE CALLS

You cannot say I didn't warn you: Trying to eliminate clutter forever is a futile effort. Your friendly postal carrier will be one of the first to remind you. Once you hit Ground Zero, you will have about fifteen seconds to shout hip hip hooray before clutter comes knocking at your door. Through wind and rain, sleet and snow, your daily mail carrier will keep his promise to deliver. God Bless America, but how do you handle the daily mail? You have shifted your perspective about your physical environment from being a victim to being in charge and have learned new skills. Now you are ready to have everything you put in place work for, instead of against, you.

An elderly woman who traveled more than two hours to attend a seminar I led on a farm in the middle of Indiana perked up during the class and said, "Oh, I see. If I clean my M-A-I-L, I will be able to have a new M-A-L-E in my life." She confided later that she had lost her husband of fifty years a few months before, and the greatest respect she could pay to the man with whom she had shared her life for so long was to move ahead in living her life fully now that she was alone.

Daily mail lets you know that you are alive. The time to worry is not when it does come, but when it doesn't. Look at it this way: All these people want to be in touch with you. Granted, some mail is from bill collectors, but other mail is in the form of postcards from friends, and even for a few seconds you can be taken far away on their adventures. Or maybe there is a check hungry to be deposited or an acceptance notice of some kind. That is to say, it's not all bad.

Begin processing mail when you walk in the door with it by putting like-kind mail together. Next, turn to your filing system. Drop all bills to be paid right into that file. While you are in the neighborhood of your financial files, slip any papers relevant to this area into the appropriate folders. If it is a bank statement, you have a place for it. If it is a frequent-flyer mileage statement, glance at the promotional inserts and toss them before putting your records away. A letter from your insurance carrier has a slot. Do the same with papers in the professional and personal areas. If an item relates to an interest that you have or a project you are already working on, most likely you have already created a file for it. If not, put it in the in-box and deal with it later. Putting it in the in-box will place it on the path of being the first paper of its kind that you create a new file for in the not-too-distant future.

Open junk mail quickly, but do not just throw it out blindly. Sometimes, it is actually something useful or even important. If you are a teacher and *National Geographic* sends you a subscription notice that has pictures of exotic animals that are good for a lesson plan you are preparing, keep the notice where your papers of that nature are, even if you do not plan to order it. Or if the pictures are good for an art project you know your child is working on at school, you can direct it to your child's attention. When you glance at an insert, add it to your in-box if it is something you want to read later. Letters that require a written response or a phone call should also be put in the in-box.

The swiftest action is always the best for announcements for a course, fund-raiser, theater event, or anything else that requires you to check your schedule and decide whether to attend. If you are interested, try to check your calendar right away to see if you are available to go. In so doing, you will know immediately if the announcement is trash or if there is something else you need to do with it. Knowing what you are making room for in your life for will make your actions easier. The opportunity will be relevant to your goals or not, making a long drawn-out decision unnecessary. There are rarely enough hours in a day to do everything, and having practice cleaning clutter will enable you to choose readily. By concentrating on your focus, you will be free to enjoy what you are doing, rather than be distracted by what you are not.

If you decide to attend a public event, mark it and relevant phone numbers on your calendar and toss the notice. Often, I like to clip the notice to the day-of-event page in my date book, but if doing so is too bulky for your system, have a file for these activities and insert notices when they arrive and pull them when you need to. If you put notices for events about which you are undecided in a file, you have to make it a habit to review this type of file with the regularity of brushing your teeth, otherwise it will be useless. Or put such a notice in a file that is related to the personal or professional interest associated with it. You can use a bulletin board to handle such notices, but the need to clean it constantly is the key to whether that practice is a waste. You can also designate a slot on your desk for invitations and events. But don't use this organizational tool to collect other kinds of stuff, too, thereby turning it to clutter.

When you are clutter free, you are likely to receive less mail that is irrelevant to you. Some may still be junk, but less of it will be when you are clutter free. This is one of the phenome- nal things about the cleaning process. What you don't want, need, or love is less likely to come your way.

Anytime something is chronically annoying, such as some junk mail, treat it as you would any clutter. Don't be angry; take action. One way to get off mailing lists is to register with the Direct Mail Marketing Association by writing to the organi- zation at the following address: Mail Preference Service, Direct Mail Marketing Association, P.O. Box 9008, Farmingdale, NY 11735–9008. This service is recommended by the U.S. Postal Service, which warns that in your letter, you should specify which catalogs you want to continue to receive. Or visit www.zerojunkmail.com. You can join this environmentally aware and privacy-conscious organization for fifteen dollars a year to get your name off thousands of mailing lists used by telemarketers, junk mailers, direct marketers, and database companies. Be diligent about getting off mailing lists; don't just be disgruntled.

There was a point when one call to a nonprofit company to request information thrust me into the cycle of all its mailings, which were inordinately frequent. After a while, I found that getting this mail was so oppressive that spending the time and effort to do something about it was a matter of well-being. It took me two months or more to get off this particular mailing list, but it was worth it because I am no longer harassed and plagued by a perpetual internal dialogue of rage and complaint.

Magazines and catalogs are inevitably part of the daily mail. Stack them together and put them in a place you designate as the one you will go to when you are ready to read them. I dis- cuss catalogs and magazines in more detail in the next two sections.

Along with handling the daily mail goes keeping up with other forms of communication you receive. Respond to tele- phone, voice mail, and E-mail messages and other communi- cations promptly—don't let them pile up. Just as not paying attention to papers or clothes that pile up turn them against you, dismissing communications with others can lead to misunderstandings and misinterpretations that close down doors.

CATALOGS

Before I went into the clutter business, I never used to get any catalogs. I know I must have been a blip on the big screen of life because everyone else in the world I know gets lots of them. Once I was introduced to the world of catalogs through my clients, I discovered how they could be useful to me. First, I saw that some catalogs sell items not easily found in stores that offer solutions to common clutter problems and thus were of professional interest to me. Second, I found that some catalogs carried clothing, linens, and home accessories and housewares that were of personal interest to me. They sold items that could round out a wardrobe, appoint my apartment, or be the off-season items I was desperate to have for a vacation. Catalogs are either a viable shopping experience or they are trash. They are either a worthy option or not, but they are never the enemy.

There are catalogs for almost every need you may have in the various areas and interests in your life, from gardening to kitchen and office supplies; from children's clothes and toys to gifts, books, and audiotapes; or for just about any hobby. Purposefully receive the ones that have something to offer you or stop them from coming. And if there are catalogs that you want to get, ask for them deliberately. Call stores and ask them to send catalogs or look up retailers' sites on the Internet to see if they have ordering services. When you begin to ask for what you want, catalogs included, you'll know you have turned the tables on clutter!

Since companies will not stop sending catalogs aggressively, handle the catalogs you receive by processing them swiftly with the daily mail. If you can, page through them immediately for what you know you need, which you will have learned in the clutter-cleaning process. If something catches your eye and you want to include it in a purchase plan, fold or clip the page and put it in a designated place for catalogs. If there is nothing you want from the catalog, toss it.

If when you collect your mail you have one foot in the door and the other in the kitchen to cook dinner, apply the path-for-everything, everything-on-its-path principle. Put catalogs on a path to their eventual destination right away (a basket might work well) before you forget about them and they become clutter.

If you need to return or exchange an item that you ordered from a catalog, do it right away. I often have seen boxes and bags for items ordered even years before leading a life of clutter in my clients' homes.

MAGAZINES, NEWSPAPERS, TELEVISION, AND MY DOCTOR'S PRESCRIPTION FOR CLUTTER

Magazines, like catalogs, don't have to be the bane of your existence. But unlike catalogs, you have to pay for magazines. Therefore, the magazines you receive are ones you have chosen, and only you are responsible if they are an annoyance.

Look to what you are making room for in your life in each coming year to inform your choice of which publications to get. If you are focusing on financial abundance, select one or two business and finance magazines or newsletters throughout the year. If you want to deepen your involvement in a hobby or interest, add a related magazine to your subscription list.

Select only the number of magazines that you can actually read each month or week. You may try ordering them all at the same time in January. Having a consistent starting date for all magazines you have chosen will prevent you from getting confused by other offers that come in with new and better rates immediately after you have just subscribed. And when telemarketers urge you to clutter your life in other ways, don't be annoyed; be surprising. When you inform them of your thoughtful approach to the products they are selling, they will respect you and stop calling.

From year to year, you can reevaluate which magazines you actually read, which you found useful in some real way, and which will be assets to your life in the following year. Keep magazines that still apply to your life in the coming year and replace magazines on subjects that are no longer a focus with those that are. For passing interests, buy single issues of magazines at a newsstand or try visiting their on-line sites as an adventure-filled option.

Being selective about the magazines you read handles about fifty percent of the clutter concerning them. Actually reading them is another potential problem.

If you can, read each magazine in a single sitting. Skip over articles that don't hold your interest. Not everything has to. Although the old you may have argued that *everything* interests you, remember that you are not the public library. The new you knows that you have more focus than that.

In the clutter-free phase, if there are articles you want to clip and save because they are pertinent to an interest or project, put them in the appropriate files. If something is not of interest to you, but you want to pass it along to a friend, slip it into an envelope, address and stamp it, and get it ready right away for the mail. Gestures such as this can be supportive of someone else's interests or projects and can nourish a professional, personal, or family relationship. Take more pleasure in what is between the pages of a magazine. If there is none, don't subscribe. If you can't read all the magazines in a single sitting, take them to the park or a beach in warm weather, or read them while warming up at a coffee shop, bundling up in bed, or curling up next to a fire in winter, and don't feel guilty reading. It is as good to relax as it is to be informed.

Treat newspapers as you do magazines. Read, clip, and toss

them. They are even less attractive than magazines when they pile up, so don't allow them to linger.

There may be times when you need a break and want to retreat from the rest of the world for a week, a month, or even longer. Give yourself permission to call a news moratorium. Treat it as stress management. Don't worry about what you have missed. The rest of the world will keep spinning, and you can pick up on who is topping the charts, winning the wars, battling it out on the Hill, or making fashion faux pas at the Oscars soon enough.

Watching television requires less of an effort than reading newspapers and magazines, which is its greatest danger. Commonly, people decide not to have a television set in their homes to prevent becoming addicted to it. I would rather integrate than eliminate this medium entirely. Selective television watching for news or a night off as a couch potato can bring you alive, but overdoing it can be deadly.

During a routine visit to my physician around the time I started my clutter-consulting business, he gave me his remedy for all kinds of clutter when he found out about my new venture. He said, "Get up early, go to bed late, and don't watch television." As always, he gave excellent treatment, in this case for a bout of common clutter.

NEW YEAR'S RESOLUTIONS AND SPRING CLEANING

A way to keep your environment aligned with the changes and movement in your life is to make time for seasonal checkups on your papers and clothes. Flag the times you want to do so by inserting notes in your date book.

The period from early December through the end of January is a good time to revamp your paper files. This is the time to create your vision for the coming year, and refurbishing your filing system with this vision in mind can be a great asset in laying out an action plan. Go through files, see if any garbage has accumulated, and rearrange and relabel them to correspond with your interests and goals for the year ahead.

The beginning of the year is a good time to wrap up financial affairs for the tax man. The sickening feeling that tax preparation may have given you in the past will be sharply reduced, and possibly eliminated, by decluttering your papers in the first place. The gnawing feeling of pending doom that compounds your dread of Uncle Sam as April 15 approaches can also be a thing of the past, since you will already be prepared.

Duplicate the file folders you need for tax purposes and replace the papers from the previous year with the clean new folders to kick off the year with a fresh start. Put tax papers on a path to being processed and never be under the pressure of a deadline again. Your accountant will appreciate it, and you can have already moved on to other things without having wasted more time worrying than handling the business at hand. Once you are finished with your papers for tax-reporting purposes, place them in expandable wallet folders (the reddish brown kind with cloth or elastic bands around them that attorneys often carry), labeled by year, and put in storage.

Prior to the change of seasons—late winter and late summer—are the obvious times to rethink and shift your wardrobe. If you live in an area in which the weather doesn't change with the seasons, you will artificially have to build in times to do so. After you have already clutter cleaned your clothes, changing the ones hanging in the primary closet on a seasonal basis will not be an ordeal. You can use the same clothes-cleaning process you did during your game plan, but the upkeep will be swifter (as fast as an hour) because there won't be so much garbage to go through. If you do so well enough in advance of the start of a season, you will have your shopping list of purchases ready and can focus on filling in what is missing. When the sun starts to shine or the snow begins to fall, you don't have to bring the rest of your life to a halt and scramble around just to get dressed.

UNPACKING FROM TRIPS AND DOING THE LAUNDRY: THE SOONER THE BETTER

How many times have I worked with clients whose duffel bags or suitcases, half unpacked from a trip taken long ago, are still lollygagging around in the spots in which they were first dumped? This is cluttering behavior.

I don't deny the desire to hold on to a few more moments of the sun and the sand you dragged in from a warm Caribbean island. But holding on to a trip of any kind for days or months afterward, in the form of an unpacked suitcase, is not going to set you free. You will earn miracle miles on the frequent decluttering plan if you unpack immediately after you come home from a trip.

When you return from almost any kind of escape, you find that life usually gets more hurried than ever. Be prepared by having nothing in the way to greet each new day, or the trip will trip you up. Put things away so you can move right ahead to the next great adventure. Having your clothes unpacked, cleaned, and ready to go makes it easier to get out the door for the next trip, too.

Vacations were out of the question for one man who attended my course because he could not justify relaxing if he left a mess behind. I knew he had succeeded in cleaning his clutter when I received a postcard from a trip he had taken. Discomfort with vacations in fear of returning to turmoil also prompted another client to clean. Now she travels spontaneously without reservation.

Laundry is another opportunity to put clothes back where they belong without hesitation. Make washing, ironing, and putting away your clothes one uninterrupted effort. Add some pleasure to doing it by combining it with an activity that you find fun or relaxing. Rent a movie you've been wanting to see and watch it between cycles. Listen to books on tape or music for your enjoyment or to lift your spirits while you iron. Another good thing to listen to while you bleach and fold are instructional tapes from experts in the areas of interest for which you are making room in your life. Also use the time as a way to slow down during a day by making a few unrushed phone calls to family members and friends.

Like unpacking from a trip, doing the laundry can be time well spent, yet the sooner you can put it behind you, the better.

13

 **Using Time Wisely**

Time is the source of great suffering for many people and is second to "peace" when it comes to what people tell me they want most as a result of cleaning clutter. They want to manage it, strive to lasso it so it does not dominate them, desire more of it.

From the clutter-free point of view, time is the quintessential structure. Regardless of how you may try to perfect your time-management skills, it is impossible to manage time. Time does not budge. It tells the sun when to rise and when to set. It is not negotiable.

To have more peace, as well as more time, start by letting go of the notion that time can be manipulated. Then, let go of the idea that it confines you. Instead, set out to use the time that is there for its true and best purpose—as the space within which you can live your life to the fullest.

Although time cannot be molded, the way you spend it can

be. The best tool for doing so is to use a date-book management system as if it was your right-hand man—both the gate-
keeper of the precious treasure of time and the shepherd
whose service to his master is to assure that the master does
not lose the way. I will discuss this idea in more detail next.

Since making the most of time is frequently addressed by
making lists of things to do and attempting to cross things off
them, I'll also discuss the questionable virtue of "to-do" lists.
The gesture of eliminating any item from a list implies that
your approach to life is to slay it, but there is a kinder, gentler
approach.

DATE BOOKS

A date-book system is another framework for freedom, giving you a good base from which to operate that will take being
clutter free from your home out into the world. Like a conduc-
tor using a baton, you can use a date book to harmonize the
boldness of your actions with the sweetness of your desires.

Some people don't keep date books, and others have too
many—a date book, wall or desk calendar, electronic organizer, or software program combination. Whether you have a
busy career, are looking for one, are retired, or are head of the
household, I recommend using one date-book system for
everything. Carry it with you at all times, with few exceptions.
If you have it as a ready reference, you can easily make commitments and avoid double-booking your time, having to get
back to someone later, or leaving things in limbo. Use your
date book to construct each day as one you really look forward to living.

Apply the skills you have learned about what to keep and
what to let go of to deciding what does and does not go into
your schedule. Use what you are making room for as a guiding
light to illuminate the best ways to spend your time for your
greatest pleasure, productivity, and fulfillment. Then see what

needs to be added. What are you *not* doing that you could be doing to move you in the direction you want to go in your life? Aligning your life and your time streamlines energy and gives you more power.

Think ahead to the things that need to get done and where you are going to be and see if you can combine some tasks. On the way to work, if you can drop off laundry, mail a letter, or deliver a bag of unwanted clothing to a shelter, do it and save yourself some steps.

As your date-book appointments take shape, pace your appointments realistically. If it takes half an hour to travel from one appointment to the next, don't leave yourself fifteen minutes. To thine own self be true. There are enough pressures in a day without the ones you impose on yourself.

You will always be tempted to move and change appointments without a second thought, but to live clutter free, you must think twice. If you create a schedule that reflects the way you want to live your life and follow it, moving in the direction you want to go will not depend on the weather, your moods, or the whims of others. Greet detours, interruptions, and roadblocks in your day by giving utmost respect to what you said you would do or by being where you had planned. Keep "emergencies" or other "unavoidable problems" to a minimum. You've learned to manage distractions to stay on your clutter-cleaning schedule. Now apply what you have learned to stay on schedule day to day. Staying on schedule may place a demand on you to communicate more effectively with others and require that you operate differently than ever before, but clutter cleaning can have this positive effect.

If there is too much stress in your day, it is a signal that something has to change. Review whether you are doing things that are irrelevant to your aims, whether you need to delegate some jobs to others, or whether you have to cut back on the number of commitments you have made.

As date books become an essential accessory, you will want

to choose one that best fits your personal style. There are all kinds of consumer electronic gizmos that organize your time and that can be used to store addresses and phone numbers as well. They are compact and portable and can be uploaded to and downloaded from your computer. I prefer them for managing names, telephone numbers, and addresses, but still prefer a paper date-book system for scheduling appointments such as the Week at a Glance date books.

Week at a Glance date books are the most basic and easy to use. The 8½ x 11-inch size gives you plenty of writing space and can easily be slipped into a tote bag or briefcase as a constant companion. When you open the Week at a Glance to a double-page spread, you really can see the week at a glance— individual columns for each day of one week with lines that delineate each hour. In addition to writing down appointments, there is plenty of room to make to-do notations or to record the numbers for telephone calls you need to make. While you may schedule things a year, a season, or a month in advance, this type of format enables you to see readily before Monday gets under way that you have a week worth living.

Other week-by-week date-book systems include Levenger in Delray Beach, Florida (800–544–0880); Quovadis in Hamburg, New York (800–535–5656); and the Seven Habits Organizer, available from the Covey Leadership Center in Provo, Utah (800–331–7716). A date book can tempt you to slip all kinds of miscellaneous papers between its covers and pages, so be sure to find other places to collect receipts, business cards, and other potential forms of clutter. When used with respect, your date book can effectively help you transform dreams into actions.

TO DO OR NOT TO DO: THE QUESTIONABLE VIRTUE OF LISTS

To-do lists are often the badges that people display as proof of how organized they are. I find them to be restrictive and a constant reminder that all you are doing is never enough. Is there any way around them?

Ordinarily, a to-do list lists chores in random order. Go grocery shopping, call Bill for a marketing meeting, sign up for the class in the continuing education program at the local high school, tally receipts, fill out the application for Johnny's nursery school, and research housing arrangements for Mom. Declutter your to-do list by putting items in like-kind groupings related to your goals. For example, if your goal is to increase your family's well-being, group finding housing accommodations for your elderly parent with filling out your child's application for nursery school. Talking to Bill about the marketing plan and tallying receipts for the accountant may both be related to your intention to increase your gross annual earnings. Going to the office supply store and resolving the dispute about telephone company charges may be part of your clutter-cleaning game plan.

If it does not interest or work for you to eliminate to-do lists entirely, try creating a one-day-at-a-time to-do list. Only list the activities you are going to do in a given day. Then, treat the list in the same way you would a pile of papers. Complete each item systematically from the top of the list to the bottom. Do not put more items on the list than you can realistically complete. A longer, more random list of actions associated with a particular interest or goal can be placed in the file you have for it and then be used as a reference for planning your daily activities.

To-do lists give you the illusion that everything about everything should get done at once, while putting things to be done in a date book makes the likelihood of accomplishing them more certain.

14

Honor Others as You Honor Yourself

On your journey through your clutter, you have voyaged to your soul—one of the most clutter-free spots of all. It is here that you are most anchored, clear on what you want, and steeped in an environment that is filled with all that is good for you. By now, your relationship with your physical universe will have been transformed. Instead of clutter being your obstacle, it has became a vehicle for change. Once you've lightened up, take time to look for more ways to stay clutter free and new areas of your life in which to apply your clutter-cleaning skills. Your inaugural journey to Ground Zero may be complete, but the opportunities to keep cleaning clutter and expanding your horizons are as endless as clutter itself.

Redirecting your clutter-cleaning efforts to other aspects of your life—emotional, mental, and spiritual—can help clear a path to balance, harmony, and fulfillment. Each effort is a way to continue the process you started—using clutter cleaning as a tool to keep the space around you open, to honor yourself, and to give you good reason to celebrate. There are two things you should never do alone—suffer and celebrate.

Most of my clients tell me that they want to clean clutter so they can entertain people in their homes. They say they don't entertain because clutter is an embarrassment. Now that you are clutter free, go ahead and celebrate by planning simple dinners with friends, hosting a holiday meal, offering your place for a community gathering, or welcoming guests even on last-minute notice. Show your appreciation for others by giving gifts in a clutter-free style and communicating clearly and effectively to keep your relationships open. You've gotten more in touch with yourself in the process of cleaning clutter. Now is a great time to clear the path to be in touch with others in more rewarding ways.

AT HOME WITH YOURSELF

Without clutter in the way, you may notice dust blanketing a bureau or dirt covering the floor. Even if everything you have stashed under the kitchen sink is something that you need and use, it may still be in disarray—signaling you to do some housekeeping.

Housecleaning is different from clutter cleaning. It is more about straightening and wiping and brushing and sweeping and scrubbing than it is about clipping and filing and hanging and tossing. Housekeeping makes a clutter-free environment sparkle. Think of housekeeping as serving to calm the energy in your space, adding to the tranquillity that most of us never seem to get enough of. Try to make your housekeeping sessions as routine as your clutter-cleaning sessions, with the same mindfulness toward moving ahead.

When you wake up, make your bed. This is a routine that can signal the start of a day and be a clutter-free spot that beckons to you at the end. At the end of a day, straighten up before you turn in.

My mother taught me by example to do a quick straightening up before going to bed. She treated turning in at night as if she was the manager of a retail store (shopping was her favorite pastime) closing up for the night. She'd check to see that the dishes were done, that magazines were back in the basket, and that everything else was in place for the new day.

When you are clutter free and your house shines, your dwelling will be your pride and you will be more at home in your world. Now, you can look for other places to apply your clutter-free skills. Even though the return on your investment in cleaning clutter will be better health and balance and greater energy, these are things that you can always use more of to stay on top of your clutter and enjoy all the new changes. Consistently giving attention to the fitness of your body, another physical environment, will help make it an instrument for living free.

There are lots of things you can do to make yourself more physically fit. The most obvious way is by eating healthy food, exercising regularly, and not smoking. In addition, you can experiment with different body-work techniques, from standard massage to one of the many eclectic varieties, to restore energy and keep it moving through your body as freely as it moves through your home. Consider it a necessity, rather than a luxury, to take a walk in nature, soak in a hot tub, sweat it out in a sauna or a steam bath, or do anything else you enjoy that will release tension and revitalize you.

If you have made the changes in your physical environment while being mindful of parallel shifts in your emotional, mental, and spiritual environments, then it may intrigue you to try clutter cleaning from a new angle. Experiment with applying your clutter-cleaning skills to any one of the other aspects of life and see how you evolve from that vantage point.

I had a clutter-cleaning client who made his living by staying in balance. When he was not employed as a clown who paraded around on stilts for parties, he was a fiddler who walked the high wire. In the course of his work, he went from performing in Central Park to appearing in *Barnum* on

Broadway. He told me that working on cleaning clutter was just like all his other jobs. He said that to keep in balance, you have to stay in constant motion. Like my client, you can keep moving forward by cleaning clutter not only in your home but in other domains in which you dwell.

For example, if your emotional environment crowds your freedom, you can take an inventory to identify what you want to make room for and apply routine practices and disciplines to alter things. If your way of thinking seems to have you stuck, pick a place to start and move along a different path. If your experience of all that is good about the human or divine spirit is stifled, schedule time in your date book to get back in touch with the joy of being alive. Keep cleaning the emotional, mental, or spiritual clutter—whatever is restraining, confining, and blocking you.

Money and sex are two of the most challenging aspects of life to declutter, but extremely worth the trouble. Money and sex wield great strength in the physical dimension of being human and power in the abstract—the emotional, mental, and spiritual aspects of life. Decluttering them may be especially difficult because all aspects of money and sex form such a tightly woven web, compounded by the fact that even today they remain to be taboo topics—often not the subject of honest communication. I would urge you, however, to give decluttering these aspects of your life a try. Really clarify who you are and what you want in these areas. Furthermore, take the action to manifest your desires. Doing so will open the space for you to enjoy two of the poignant experiences of being clutter free—the true abundance of knowing and loving yourself and sharing freely and openly with others.

CELEBRATING YOUR RELATIONSHIPS WITH OTHERS

Sending thank-you notes and returning telephone calls promptly are ways to keep cleaning your clutter and to share the virtues of clutter cleaning with others. If you carry through with your intention to show courtesy or appreciation, you will not only turn clutter into finished business, but you will show others that you care.

Giving gifts is always an occasion to let more grace abound in your environment—but gifts too can also become clutter. To avoid spreading clutter, give people what they really want, what will really make them—not you—happy. When in doubt, ask them. This type of gift giving is an expression of your clutter-free consciousness.

Some families exchange wish lists on holidays and special occasions. More and more retail marketers are offering gift registries for all kinds of occasions, not just weddings. You can register for everything from Christmas and birthday gifts, to graduation and Mother's Day or Father's Day presents. If you don't want to receive gifts that are clutter, consider asking for more of what you want from others. Ask your friends and family members to understand how giving you what you want will help you stay clutter free.

Gifts are one way to toast your relationship with others; having them as guests in your home is another. Among the leading reasons why people say they want to clean their clutter is so they can entertain. If clutter is stopping you from entertaining, entertaining is one of the best motivations for cleaning it.

Clutter cleaning can enrich your involvement with others because you will want to welcome them into your sacred space—your home—afterward. Some clutterers, when they dare to entertain, stuff whatever is unsightly into a bag and jam it into a closet. Resist this temptation—you'll know the bag is in the closet, and you'll feel less free to enjoy your guests.

One client had never hosted Passover in her home because of her clutter. Even though Heather is a Jew of the Orthodox tradition, which is strict about following customs, she had never been willing to host the seder. Proper preparation for the holiday meal entails following stringent laws that include taking extraordinary measures to clean the home thoroughly. Such cleaning was especially daunting for Heather, not only because she had clutter but because she had been taught as a child that if she did not abide by the laws of her faith, she risked spiritual estrangement. Heather began one of her clutter-cleaning sessions wondering why she was now willing to host the Passover seder and how it related to cleaning clutter.

Since asking the question "why" is part of the Passover tradition, I answered the question in the spirit of the occasion: "It is appropriate that on a holiday that commemorates the flight to freedom of the Jewish people, that you are now liberated to practice your faith. Perhaps clutter cleaning is one of the ways for us to see how God moves in funny ways. Maybe cleanliness is next to Godliness!" Heather agreed that clutter cleaning made her feel more liberated, confident that she could be abiding to her faith, and more mature.

If you are living clutter free and guests give you short notice of their arrival, you can be spontaneous and accommodating by welcoming them without a fuss.

At other times there may be opportunities that come your way to host meetings or gatherings in your home. Whereas you previously may have avoided those situations, now that you are clutter free, consider jumping at the chance. This is not only a time to give yourself more, not less, of what you want, it can be an inducement to return to Ground Zero more frequently than you otherwise might.

During the decluttering process, you got in touch with yourself. A key to living clutter free is to be more in touch with others. Keep the channels of communication open and keep clutter from being in the way of your relationships with others. Minding your manners, reaching out, and sharing who you are can make a cruel world more kind.

The End

Just like clutter consultations and classes, it is time for this book to come to an end. You have new skills under your belt and a few ideas on how to live clutter free. Instead of having all the papers, clothes, and other things in your life impeding your way, you are well equipped to get them moving in the same direction that you want to go in. In the course of combing through these pages, I hope you have transformed from being a mouse under all that clutter to Mighty Mouse on top of the heap (of your life, not your stuff)!

Even though your destiny is in your own hands now, if you still need help from a friend, another teacher, a private consultant, or me to keep up your courage and get a little wind beneath your cape, don't hesitate to ask for it. As long as you don't look at any assistance as a magical solution that will make clutter instantly disappear, getting support to stay on track is anything but cowardly.

First, become a student of the things that you learned in this book. Try the exercises, practice the principles, create a game plan, and begin to execute the plan to see how it can work wonders for you. Keep the book as a companion during the process and, as I suggested at the beginning, read it through once, refer to specific chapters as needed, review the At-a-Glance sections, and flip to any page at the start of each session just for the fun of it. Use your clutter-cleaning journal.

In addition, you can visit the Lighten Up! Free Yourself from Clutter website at www.freefromclutter.com for news and information. If you would like to be put on the Lighten Up! Free Yourself from Clutter mailing list, I'll take it to mean you are serious about wanting to get updates on clutter-cleaning news that may be of interest. All daily mail is not bad, and I don't send things to clients often. So, should something arrive from me, you'll know I think that it is worth your while. You can send your name, address, and telephone number to: Lighten Up! Free Yourself from Clutter, Cathedral Station, P.O. Box 1838, New York, NY 10025.

Also, look for classes at continuing education institutions in your area on clutter, organization, interior design, or topics that are related to living clutter free. They can help you expand your knowledge, give you various techniques, and keep you focused on your clutter-cleaning process. Other books and tapes on clutter and related subjects can offer different points of view and additional information, too.

Professional help with clutter is becoming increasingly available throughout the country. Check advertisements in your local newspapers for services that are offered in your area. You can also telephone the referral line of the National Association of Professional Organizers at (512) 206–0151, E-mail the association at NAPO@assmngmt.com, or visit its website on the Internet. If you hire a consultant, I would urge you not to rely on the consultant to clean your clutter for you. Think of the consultant as a trainer to help kick-start the process and teach you what he or she knows. But in the end, it is still best to have your own clutter-cleaning policies.

I know from the messages I get on my answering machine and the notes I receive in the mail from clients, students, and even their relatives that clutter can subside and that lighter, more moving moments in your life can take its place.

For example, I received a telephone message from one client who said, "Hi, just sitting here cleaning out my pocketbook and thinking of you. Thought I'd give you a call to say hello!" The human comedy of clutter often makes me laugh.

Or how about the message from the woman who boasted, "I found a perfect three-drawer lateral file at a secondhand store and spent the last couple of days typing 130 labels. That should cover every possible aspect of my life. I wanted to let you know that I made a tremendous breakthrough." This woman had spent one year doing whatever it took to get to a clutter class, and this call came six months after she had already attended. Her will to break free was inspiring.

I received a note from the sister of a client thanking me for teaching her sibling to clean. The client had visited her sister and helped clear her and her daughter's clutter. I saw this clutter cleaning as an act of sisterly love. When another client told me of her travels to a distant city to help her son clean his clutter in an emergency, I saw clutter cleaning as an act of motherly love. For every client with whom I have worked, I have seen the process of cleaning clutter as an act of self-love.

As you clean your clutter, you will see whatever *you* see. Just remember: When it comes to clutter, there is more than meets the eye. You have my sincere wishes that what you have is only the best of everything. Since clutter never ends, I will not take this occasion to say good-bye. I bid you a fond farewell for now.

Living Clutter Free At a Glance

- When you have reached Ground Zero and your surroundings are free of clutter, you can seek clutter before it finds you. Look for new ways to clean whatever is obstructing the range of freedom you want to enjoy.

- Routinely handle the daily mail, use catalogs as a resource to get what you want, and subscribe to magazines that support your goals. Be disciplined about spring cleaning, unpacking from trips, and doing laundry in a timely manner.

- Use time wisely. Let go of the idea that it confines you. Instead, use it for its true and best purpose—as the space within which you can live your life fully. Have one date-book system that goes with you everywhere. Use it to design a schedule that corresponds to what you are making room for in your life and that you look forward to following.

- Housekeeping at regularly scheduled times can not only help you keep the space you created open, but make it sparkle. Make your bed in the morning and straighten up before you turn in at night so you don't trip over clutter the next day. Declutter emotional, mental, and spiritual realms as a way to continue to honor yourself and be more at home in your world.

- Celebrate your relationships with others. Welcome guests in your clutter-free home. Write thank-you notes and return telephone calls promptly. This part of cleaning clutter keeps the lines of communication open and makes a cruel world more kind.

- **Continue to learn new skills and stay focused on your cleaning process by taking related courses or hiring a personal consultant. If you want to be on the Lighten Up! Free Yourself from Clutter mailing list to receive updates (only essential ones, so you don't get more mail than you can use), send your name, address, and telephone number to: Lighten Up! Free Yourself from Clutter, Cathedral Station, P.O. Box 1838, New York, NY 10025 or visit www.freefromclutter.com.**

Index